GW00385339

Violence and Anarchism

FREEDOM PRESS CENTENARY SERIES

Supplement to Volume 4, *Selections From Freedom 1951-1964*

Published by
FREEDOM PRESS
84b Whitechapel High Street
London E1 7QX

© FREEDOM PRESS

ISBN 0 900384 70 0

Printed in Great Britain by
Aldgate Press, 84b Whitechapel High Street, London E1 7QX

VIOLENCE
& ANARCHISM

A Polemic

Edited by
Vernon Richards

FREEDOM PRESS
LONDON
1993

FREEDOM PRESS publishes *Freedom* fortnightly, *The Raven* quarterly, and anarchist books and pamphlets (currently seventy titles in print).

Freedom is a propaganda newspaper, commenting on world affairs from an anarchist point of view. The first edition appeared in October 1886. Its style has always been discursive, seeking to disseminate anarchism by getting anarchist ideas discussed by readers outside the anarchist movement.

The Raven is a quarterly magazine of 96 pages, dealing with anarchist ideas at greater length. Recent issues have included collections of essays on Anthropology, Sociology and Use of the Land.

Freedom Press has published books and pamphlets for more than a century. These include classic and recent statements of the anarchist case, history books, hilarious cartoon books, and anarchist treatments of particular aspects of life. The Anarchist Discussion series was begun in 1991.

Freedom Press Bookshop, open six days a week, also sells works of anarchist interest from commercial and academic publishers, across the counter and by mail order. The shop entrance is in Angel Alley, a long passage approached by a pedestrian tunnel, alongside the Whitechapel Art Gallery.

Send for a free specimen copy of *Freedom* and a list of over 400 titles, most of them post free:

Freedom Press, 84b Whitechapel High Street, London, E1 7QX.

Contents

Anarchist Violence

There is no greater error than to believe that we, as anarchists, need only to commit *any* deed, no matter *when, where* and against *whom.* To have a propaganda effect, every deed needs to be *popular;* it must meet with approval by an important part of the proletariat. If that is not the case, or if it actually meets with the *disapproval* of the very part of the population it is intended to inspire ... anarchism makes itself unpopular and hated. Instead of winning new adherents, many will withdraw.

Johannes Most (1888)

(Quoted by H. Becker in *The Haymarket Scrapbook*)

Editor's Introduction

In March 1960 a demonstration called for by the Pan-African Congress, in protest against the pass laws, took place in Sharpeville, a township near Vereeniging. The violence used by the police against the non-violent protesters was said to have 'shocked' hard-bitten South African newsmen and even some of the police. Fifty six Africans - men, women and children - were killed by the police; some 160 were injured.

The Pan-African Congress was described at the time as 'an extremist break-away' of the African National Congress (ANC) and had called on its 31,000 members in the Union to come out *without* their passes. At Sharpeville the crowd grew to 20,000 strong and surrounded the police station, shouting. According to *Reuter*, one African was shot dead and four injured after the police had been stoned. The Africans retaliated and the police opened fire after attempts to intimidate and disperse them by the use of aircraft diving low over the area, and Saracen armoured cars (which, incidentally, had been sold to the South African government by the British Armaments industry) forcing their way through the crowd to take up defensive positions by the police station. But those provocative actions only angered the crowd still further. The local area police commander, Colonel J. Piernaar was reported as saying: 'I don't know how many we shot. It all started when hordes of natives surrounded the police station. My car was struck by a stone. If they do these things they must learn their lesson the hard way'. The police commander's 'hard way' in retaliation for stones, including the one that struck his car, was: 56 dead and 160 injured - all black.

Dr Verwoerd and his white government had won the day. The 10 to 1 black majority retired defeated: their stones no match for Verwoerd's machine guns, *until* a white man, David Pratt, did what no black man dared to do, and shot at the mastermind of Apartheid in South Africa, the symbol of white supremacy and all the injustices, the exploitation of native labour that had existed from the moment the white colonists had invaded the African continent. Verwoerd survived and, as editorial writer for *Freedom* (weekly) at that time, I expressed my disappointment with an editorial, 'Too Bad He Missed'. That particular issue of *Freedom* (April 16, 1960) coincided with an Aldermaston march organised by the CND at which the anarchists had marchers and literature sellers (who could count on selling up to 1,000 copies of *Freedom* and other literature over the four days march).

Little did I realise that the editorial would ruffle so many pacifist feathers, among those readers of *Freedom* who considered themselves as anarchists. They did not go as far as the Queen, and the then Prime Minister (Mr Macmillan) or even the leader of the Labour Party to send telegrams of sympathy to Verwoerd but not to the relatives of the victims of Sharpeville, but for them our editorial had blotted the anarchists' copy-book — or at least *Freedom's*.

Since the violence — non-violence issue among anarchists shows no signs of abating over the years (as evidenced in *Freedom* in the last year or so) it seemed to me worthwhile to reproduce the polemic of 1960 as a supplementary volume in the Freedom Centenary Series for the years 1951-1964. No editing either of the editorials or the correspondence has been made.

In addition I have included as an appendix Martyn Everett's *Short History of Political Violence in Britain* just as a reminder of how the State, even in a so-called democracy, reacts even when opposed non-violently and a second appendix of Malatesta's writings on *Attentats* and on *Anarchism and Violence* written in the early 1920s when revolution was in the air in post-World War I Europe as well as nascent fascism.

Vernon Richards

Editorial

Too Bad He Missed

The general chorus of righteous indignation with which the wonderful news that someone at last had decided it was time to eliminate the racialist butcher Dr. Verwoerd, has been received in the Press and in official circles in this country, was to be expected. The Queen, who as far as we know said nothing when 91 African men, women and children were shot down in cold blood by Verwoerd's police, duly sent her sympathy telegram; Mr. Macmillan who could not be persuaded to protest in the name of the government over the shootings at Sharpeville also produced the standard condolences cable, and the Leader of the Opposition though he didn't go to the lengths of emulating the Prime Minister, who assured his shot counterpart that he and Mrs M 'are both thinking of you very much', nevertheless issued a statement in which he declared that:

Whatever the circumstances and despite the Labour Party's strong disapproval of the South African Government's racial policies, I deeply regret that this attack should have been made upon Dr. Verwoerd.

The Press as a whole was even more sickly in its editorial expressions of horror. The *News Chronicle* which only a few days before had featured on its front page a dispatch from correspondent Stephen Barber, in which he described the indiscriminate terror which had been unleashed by the police against all Africans they found in the streets, refers to the attempt as 'deplorable' and the impact of the first news as 'appalling'. Like the *Guardian* ('We must be profoundly thankful') this voice of Liberalism was relieved to learn that the unsuccessful assassin was not an African.

The Tory *Daily Telegraph* on the other hand which views that attempt with 'revulsion' also considers it 'senseless' and fears that it may 'bring new bitterness between white South Africans'. 'Had

9

Dr. Verwoerd's assailant been a black African' declares the *Daily Telegraph* 'that would have been understandable'. We wonder whether that would have been the editorial line if in fact the assailant had been a 'black African'!

The Times from its lofty heights editorialises on 'A Dreadful Act'.

This is a moment at which all men of good will - Africaner and English, white, coloured and black - pause in a spirit of mutually shared horror.

What a lot of nonsense! Reports from Johannesburg pointed out that in spite of the shooting the people attending the Agricultural Fair went on enjoying themselves on the roundabouts and swings as if nothing had happened! And we agree for once, with Cassandra of the *Daily Mirror* when he wrote on Monday that

In fact such is the bitterness in the minds of the British public that when the news came through on Saturday afternoon there were expressions of everything from satisfaction to pleasure - but no regret.

How wrong is *The Times* when it suggests that 'An assassin has no friends; his dreadful act points no moral; it comes simply as a heart-breaking reminder of the infinite fallibility of human nature'.

Millions of people throughout the world disgusted by the racial policies of the South African government will have read the news of the attempt on Verwoerd with disappointment only because the attempt failed. For them, David Pratt did what they had neither the opportunity nor, in the event, the courage, to do. Of course assassination is a desperate act, and we know that the elimination of Verwoerd would not have removed the basic problems which divide the people of South Africa. But who will deny that it is the only language that dictators and tyrants understand? Verwoerd has escaped with his life, but we suggest that if he returns to lead the government what happened to him last Saturday will influence his future policy and the way he seeks to carry it out. If he decides to retire then those who succeed him will be chastened by the thought that what might have happened to their predecessor might well happen to them.

A society such as that in South Africa, in which the majority is denied the most elementary rights by the ruling minority, can only be maintained by the use of naked violence. Throughout its history the black African has invariably been the victim. Last Saturday's news made a pleasant change. And in sending our condolences and solidarity to David Pratt, who for his gesture is to be detained indefinitely under the Emergency Laws, we express the hope that no dictator, be he black, white or coloured; in Africa, Spain, South America or on either side of the curtain of power, will now sleep in peace!

April 16, 1960

Tony Smythe

'A Crumbling Monument to the Bad Old Days'?

Comrades,

The editors of FREEDOM can be commended on producing a remarkably good issue, calculated to draw new blood into the anarchist movement, for the Aldermaston March. The article on the Verwoerd shooting was therefore nothing less than a tragedy. Amid a positive wealth of basic anarchist thought it stood alone, a crumbling monument to the bad old days, a perfect example of what anarchism is not. Before the new reader had had time to discard the conventional picture of a bearded bomb-thrower in dark glasses the vision was restored with cartoon clarity.

For those selling the paper it was a constant embarrassment, all the more so if they happened to be selling *Peace News* also. I do not like to be apologetic about what I am selling but I was constantly forced to do so.

Although I consider pacifism and anarchism not only to be compatible, but also to be dependent upon each other I am well aware that not all comrades are committed to non-violence. How they reconcile individual freedom wtih assassination I do not know but surely this difference of opinion ought to be fought out in the comparatively sheltered atmosphere of the usual four page edition.

Socialists and especially Trotskyists applaud and subscribe to the 'too bad he missed' attitude but the anarchist's job is not to encourage left-wing fascists, rather to try and educate by offering better methods to attain a balanced and enlightened society.

Compassion for the wrong-doer as well as for those who have suffered oppression is a desirable although admittedly difficult ideal. In the real class struggle it is not people we are fighting but the wrong ideas. It is a mistake to assume that by eliminating individuals we can improve a situation however difficult, for violence will inevitably breed more violence and we shall end up by being as culpable as those whom we are seeking to defeat. Verwoerd's policy of apartheid is despicable and must be fought by all the non-violent means within our power but we should be able to spare pity for a man with blood streaming down his face, his wife at his side. We can express pity and understanding for the man who did the shooting, he is probably suffering for it now, and at the same time abhor the barbarity of political assassination.

When we attack the pious attitudes of press and politicians in this country we have ample justification. The ruling class obviously does not like to see one of its members dealt with in the manner which it has itself perfected. James Cameron in the *News Chronicle* was near the mark when he contrasted the reaction to the Sharpeville massacre with the eulogies which would have appeared if Verwoerd had died from his wounds.

Perhaps the editor would like to carry his ideas to their logical conclusion by assassinating Macmillan? After all he managed to give the South Africans the most telling form of encouragement, cash. I quote from the *Natal Mercury*, April 9th: 'The strategically astute move of the British Exchequer in making a handsome taxation gift to the South African wine industry'. Verwoerd is merely a figurehead, the economic blow of an efficient boycott is more effective than his removal.

Fraternally,
T.S.

London, April 20

Editorial

In Defence of David Pratt

During the Aldermaston weekend a number of shocked readers of FREEDOM assured us that we should certainly be hearing from them on the subject of our article 'Too Bad He Missed'! To date we have received one letter which is printed in the correspondence columns of this issue. That people who feel strongly about something cannot even take the trouble to voice their protest is disappointing. But might it perhaps be that our critics had second thoughts about our offending article, and are not so shocked after all? Perhaps we will manage to provoke them to speak up this week!

For months the press has been full of news of South Africa, and the Left and the Liberals have been waxing indignant about the brutal treatment meted out to those Africans who have dared to join together in protest against the policy of apartheid and racial discrimination. Pacifists, New Leftists, Communists and Socialists in this country have been boycotting South African oranges and some of them for a few days after the Sharpeville massacre made a mild nuisance of themselves (so far as the *British* authorities are concerned, that is) on the pavement outside South Africa House in London. They deplored Britain's abstention at the United Nations' debate on South Africa and many demanded that Verwoerd should be banned from the Commonwealth Ministers' meeting in London next month.

Then something happened which paralysed their brains and left them speechless. David Pratt, a wealthy farmer who keeps cattle and breeds trout for the luxury market of Johannesburg, shot Dr. Verwoerd at close range with the obvious intention of killing him. That a white South African, a wealthy man, whose wealth and status might well depend on the successful conclusion of Dr. Verwoerd's apartheid policies, should have been prepared to risk his life or at least his liberty; to exchange his material comforts (which by all accounts were considerable) for confinement in a prison cell, in order to make his protest against Verwoerd and his policies seems to us so unusual, so praiseworthy, that no one professing to radical ideas could possibly *ignore* the action even if he disagreed with the *method*. Yet this in fact is what has happened, and when we wrote our piece we knew this would be the spineless, cowardly reaction of the left, and purposely, in the headline and in the text, did our best to shock and provoke those of our readers who might have wished us to soft-peddle the whole business.

We quoted in our original piece from the Daily Press, which was unanimous in deploring the act. We did not quote from the *Daily Worker* because, apart from briefly reporting the facts, the organ of the CP *has not said one word editorially*! Of the weeklies the *New Statesman* dismisses the matter in four lines:

The gun attack on Dr. Verwoerd has had the immediate effect of reuniting almost all leading white opinion behind the traditional South African segregation policy.

The *Spectator* draws the same conclusion but is at least frank enough to admit that

The first reaction ... must be surprise that it did not happen a long time ago. No dictatorship can behave in the brutal and bloody way that his [Verwoerd's] has been doing without eventually leading someone to the conclusion that the simplest way to topple the tyrant is to shoot him dead.

Tribune relegates its short comment to the back page and though it makes clear in a roundabout way that it has no sympathy for Verwoerd, makes no attempt to understand or to explain the significance of David Pratt's gesture which it dismisses with

Assassination is an ineffective political weapon. *Tribune* does not hold the view that it is possible to shoot *apartheid* out of South Africa by shooting Verwoerd.

Not one of these journals ever mentions David Pratt by name. Of the minority weeklies we see, the *Socialist Leader* organ of the ILP has a paragraph which simply says that the *attentat* will 'tend to strengthen temporarily the National Party government by making Verwoerd into a kind of martyr - whatever the motive for the shooting, at the time of writing not revealed'. But even this cautious line was bettered by *Peace News* organ of the Peace Pledge Union by the simple expedient of ignoring it altogether. It just didn't happen!

The only honourable exception to this catalogue of moral and political cowardice is the Comment in the *Observer* (17.4.60) which we print in full:

Personal sympathy for Dr. Verwoerd, who is recovering from an attempt on his life, should be expressed and felt. He carries huge responsibilities and has no doubt done only what he believes to be right. But this should not prevent us from feeling some sympathy for Mr. David Pratt, his would-be assassin, who presumably also did what he believed to be right.

Political assassination is undoubtedly a crime in civilised communities. However, only pacifists have reproached those who made attempts on the lives of Hitler, Mussolini, Stalin and Franco, because these rulers had practised such extravagant injustice and violence themselves.

Dr. Verwoerd has placed his fellow countrymen in a situation where millions of them have no constitutional means whatsoever of expressing their political disagreements with his Government. He is driving them towards the use of violence. Every effort should be made to stop him. But if he does not treat his governed more fairly, we should not view them and him without regard to who has been hurting whom. To treat victims and oppressors as morally the same is moral nonsense.

That the *New Statesman* should dismiss the 'gun attack' in four lines does not surprise us. That journal has been politically dead for decades and it would be asking too much to expect a spark of imagination and political unorthodoxy to shake the sobriety of the columns of this self-appointed organ of the Establishment. But the silence of *Peace News* is cowardly and dishonest. We are sorry to have to say this since we esteem that journal's editor personally, but what other conclusions can we draw when it not only devotes considerable space to the struggle in Africa, but also advocates direct action, civil disobedience and 'personal witness' - all non-violent - as essential if we are to achieve the goal of a world at peace and in which all men are free and equal. 'But David Pratt's action was violent and we advocate only non-violent action' we shall be told. That is true, and we would therefore understand if *Peace News* published a denunciation of David Pratt's attempt on Dr. Verwoerd. But why the suppression? Not surely because it was an example of the violence of man. The Sharpeville massacre and many other examples of colonial violence are frequently reported and commented on in *Peace News*. We suspect they have no answer which they themselves can believe, to a gesture such as that of David Pratt. Let us analyse his gesture before we proceed further.

We know very little about David Pratt apart from the fact that he was wealthy, that he lived in style, that he was a farmer and a factory owner. He has also been described as an 'eccentric'; we have also read that he was an epileptic.

In the *Evening Standard* for April 11 there is a photograph of him with a Liberal candidate, during the last general election, taken outside 10 Downing Street. He was canvassing for the Liberal candidate for Westminster, Mr. Bute Hewes, so presumably his politics were Liberal. Mr. Hewes interviewed after the *attentat* said

I think it is wrong to write Mr. Pratt off as a madman. He was not the sort of chap to go around shouting 'down with Verwoerd'. He would go and do something about it. He helped us a great deal with door-to-door canvassing. He didn't talk very much, but he struck me as being perfectly sane.

We know nothing further either about Mr. Pratt or his motives in attempting the life of Dr. Verwoerd because on the one hand after the *Evening Standard* there has been complete silence about him in the British Press and on the other, the South African government, which had the powers to put him on trial has chosen instead to use its Emergency Powers to keep him in prison, incommunicado, without charging him or putting him on trial. The fact that such a course has been taken is, to our minds, clear evidence that it suits the government's interest not to put him on trial in open court. The reasons we can think of for this course of action are (a) that he has been so ill-treated that he is not in a fit condition to be seen by the eyes of the world Press, (b) that if he were put on trial he would defend his action along the lines of the *Observer* Comment and so win world opinion to his side whatever the criminal courts might decide to do with him as an individual, (c) that he is being brain-washed *à la Russe* and will in due course be put on trial and confess that he was instigated by the British

South Africans, or by the business men more interested in the stock markets than in the purity of the (white) stock.

On the other hand were he insane, or had the government any evidence to show that he was a member of some subversive group he would, in our opinion, now be standing trial for the attempted assassination of Verwoerd, since it would be in the government's interest to do so. We think that everything points to the David Pratt attentat as one of those unexpected gestures from a member of the privileged class (and in this case, race) who does not reject the material comforts which it allows him but who at the same time has a conscience which prevents him from rationalising his privileged status.

Unlike the *Socialist Leader* which will not commit itself until it has evidence in black and white of the motives behind the *attentat*, we accept David Pratt's action as courageous, generous and important to the future of South Africa. The Press sighed with relief that the hand behind the gun was white; for had it been black the repression that would have followed would have made Sharpeville a mere picnic. We do not share this timorous approach (how many Sharpevilles will the Press and the Left and the pacifists witness before they allow the worm to turn?) but we welcome the fact that Verwoerd's would-be assassin was white. And for quite different reasons!

Now *Peace News*, we are sure, shares our view that the only *satisfactory* solution to the South African problem is one which recognises the equal rights of all, irrespective of racial difference. For Africans to talk of driving the whites into the sea is as barbarous as the Verwoerds who seek to force the Africans into 'native reserves'. The intransigence of the white ruling class fosters a similar intransigence among the black Africans which is understandable but which our deep sympathies for their cause must not prevent us from expressing as harmful. For it not only encourages a racialism which we seek to abolish, but makes those concerned in the struggle blind to the fact that among the whites of South Africa and outside, there are many who do not assess a person's worth by the pigment of his skin. This surely is the most important aspect of David Pratt's gesture. By it he has shown the black South Africans that there are whites whose sense of justice transcends considerations of race or class. Equally, we suggest, that for those anti-racial white South Africans who have despaired of ever convincing their black brothers and sisters of their sincerity, David Pratt's gesture has been invaluable.

Finally, it has given the ruling clique in South Africa a feeling of insecurity. Verwoerd has often boasted: 'I never allow myself the luxury of ever doubting whether I might be wrong'. We may be wrong, but we strongly believe that if Verwoerd does once again take his place as, to quote Colin Legum of the *Observer*, 'the most powerful Nationalist figure in the country', he will, as a result of David Pratt's gesture, allow himself the 'luxury' of doubt.

The massacre of Sharpeville in itself is meaningless, just one more incident in the hard struggle for survival. But it has meaning when it sparks off a campaign of civil disobedience (e.g. mass burning of passes), general strikes, world opinion and yes, we submit, and pacifists must recognise it, such rare, meaningful phenomena as a David Pratt. But whereas *Peace News* has publicised Sharpeville, it has failed to recognise the relation between it and David Pratt, or that Sharpeville *needed* a David Pratt to save the dignity of mankind.

What is the pacifists' non-violent resistance? Is it a tactic, or a respect for human life as being sacrosanct? If we have understood them, it is the latter. In which case, if someone threatens to take my life am I entitled to defend it even at the expense of taking the life of my aggressor? Why if life is sacrosanct should I consider *my* life less sacrosanct than that of my aggressor? And even assuming that I consider our lives equally sacrosanct how do I resolve the problem that my aggressor does not share my view and is intent on killing me? By letting him kill me, and hoping that he will give me time to utter a little Christian homily which will plague him for the rest of his life?

In South Africa, the pacifist must recognise that the multi-racial solution will take a long time and that in the meantime the government will not hesitate to order its security forces to open fire on gatherings of citizens who threaten its authority (even non-violently). Without suggesting the use of violence to further our objectives - we agree that violence breeds violence - what is the argument for denying the individual's right to *defend* himself, if needs be by having recourse to force? To answer this question is to answer the last sentence of the *Observer*'s Comment: 'To treat victims and oppressors as morally the same is moral nonsense'. This is the pacifists' dilemma, and when David Pratt reminded them of it with his generous gesture, instead of recognising it and saluting him, they behaved as if neither existed.

We refuse to let the self-named 'direct actionists' pass by David Pratt!

April 30, 1960

Tony Gibson

A Pacifist Viewpoint on Assassination

Three weeks ago, FREEDOM published an Editorial article entitled 'Too Bad He Missed', commenting on the attempted assassination of Verwoerd by David Pratt. This has been the subject of a letter of protest by one reader, and I gather that others have been shocked by it. This is an issue which is extremely critical, involving as it does so much personal emotional feeling on the part of many people, and I therefore think that it is one on which individual's personal viewpoints are very much in order.

In publishing the article with its provocative, uncompromising title 'Too Bad He Missed' the Editors of FREEDOM have faced an issue highly dangerous for an intelligent anarchist paper, honestly and courageously. I honour them for it. Alone among the intelligent papers FREEDOM and the *Observer* published honest comment.

Obviously the politic thing for FREEDOM to have done was to evade the issue. Those who see the awful implications of an anarchist paper condoning assassination may well consider that an awful, tremendous blunder has been committed. 'And what a time to drop such a brick!' they may say; for the article was published in the double-issue selling an extra 1,500 (?) to the Liberals, Pacifists, etc. on the Aldermaston March. And on the front page too!

If the uninformed know nothing else about anarchists it is that they are reputed to throw bombs and assassinate people. Against this stigma the anarchist movement has long had to wage a patient campaign of education to show people what anarchism really stands for. There is an age-old cry that we should change the name 'anarchism' to something more 'respectable' in order to sell our goods. Viewing such of the history of the movement in this country as is known to me, I am sure sticking to the traditional name of our movement has not been a mistake. Those who have retired from the movement because it was not sufficiently 're-spectable' have been no loss, and indeed the uncompromising title protects the movement to some extent from too close an identifica-tion with that genre of anarchist fellow travellers who have one hopeful foot on the Establishment ladder.

By not evading the issue of Pratt's attempted assassination of Verwoerd, by not taking refuge in a diplomatic tut-tutting over the incident, FREEDOM can retain the respect of its readers, and further-more, it shows that it does not attempt to sell itself to new readers under false colours.

When the news of the attempted assassination was in the Sun-day papers, I was at a respectable gathering of professional people. As they sat around after breakfast reading the *Sunday Times*, the *Sunday Express* and the *Observer*, I heard their comments. 'Too bad he missed', is a fair statement of the verbally expressed opinions. One venerable professor reading the *Sunday Times* merely remarked that it was a pity the man didn't use a larger calibre revolver. All this was spoken comment at the not-too-public gathering, yet I venture to think that if the newspapers had printed the sentiments these gentlemen were freely expressing, they would have protested at such honest human sentiment appearing in print.

Why is it accepted that a certain humbug is proper in print?

I have titled this 'A Pacifist Viewpoint' because I think I should describe my general viewpoint as pacifist. Pacifism involves both emotional and intellectual factors. Emotionally I have such a strong objection to killing off the poor mutts who are regularly rounded up and equipped to slaughter one another for this cause or that, that I shall always take good care to evade the role of killer. Repugnance and cussedness are so combined in me that one day I might even foolishly lose my own dear life in obstinately evading the killer's role; but that would be an unhappy accident and not a matter of principle. Intellectually I know all the arguments for participation in an emancipatory armed struggle like the Spanish revolution. But I am unconvinced, I do not see how the Spanish tragedy could have been avoided, the participants feeling as they did. But those who pinned their faith to the armed struggle, even had they met with military success, were in my opinion, making a fundamental mistake.

However, this is not the point I wish to make. Having roughly indicated my pacifism in these matters, I can go on to say that of all forms of killing, assassination seems to me most justifiable. The soldiers who kill one another act completely irresponsibly; by delegating their own personal responsibility to their commanders they shelve their humanity. If they killed out of some honest personal hatred or vindictiveness they would have some shred of human justification. In times of war governments try to work up psychopathic hatred of 'the enemy' but it is pretty phoney and the troops know they are faced by poor mutts like themselves. Whether they kill the people of Eastasia today to support Westasia, and Westasia tomorrow to support Eastasia, it is all one. Here many comrades may remind me that revolutionary fighters know what they are fighting for, whom they are fighting and why. They have my greater sympathy but I fear that even the foregoing is not quite true, and part of the Spanish tragedy was that idealism was made to serve some pretty stinking ends.

The assassin at least acts on his own responsibility. However wrongheaded he may be he is in a different category to the soldier, and his act does not merit the contempt that the soldier's act of duty merits. The assassin must bear the consequences of his act both physically and morally; he cannot hide behind the skirts of any military command and claim to be personally blameless for his act.

Here I must sacrifice all title to be considered a pacifist, in the eyes of some. For I will not condemn each and every act of assassination. Indeed, I believe that every person of integrity and courage might have the potentiality of being an assassin if he found himself in very special circumstances. This is no mere romanticism on my part; I think it is echoed by every person who felt 'Too bad he missed', when he read how Pratt failed to kill Verwoerd.

I think it is foolish for the writer to FREEDOM (T.S.) to say 'Perhaps the editor would like to carry his ideas to their logical conclusion by assassinating Macmillan?' To do such a thing would be as crazy as it was for poor Czolgosz to kill President McKinley Crazy, because one would have to live in a very unreal private world ever to pick on Macmillan. But the world of South Africa is very different from ours; I know next to nothing about David Pratt, and it may be that he is as mad as a hatter - but that does not follow from his act. For a Marxist, the motivation which led Pratt, a rich and economically secure white man to kill the politician who was defending his class interests against the black proletariat, is quite meaningless. But there are forces beyond those which are covered by a Marxist interpretation of society. That a privileged class can exist in a condition of such un-freedom in spite of its material luxury is a fact that has produced many revolutionaries of note, and can drive men like Pratt to acts of desperation.

In refusing to condemn every act of assassination with horror, I think it fair to add that I and all responsible anarchists that I have known, have been entirely satisfied that the development of anarchism in this century has been away from acts of sporadic violence against individual despots. In actual fact the part that anarchists have played in the history of assassinations has been very small. But it is one thing to reject assassination as a feasible or permissible policy, and another to hold up pious hands in horror when a monster like Verwoerd becomes one of the minor casualties in the policy of violence and terror he is pursuing. When the man is Verwoerd I just cannot find myself 'able to spare pity for a man with blood streaming down his face, his wife at his side': to that extent my heart has been hardened. It may have been utterly impolitic to shoot at Verwoerd just now, for reasons T.S. and others have mentioned - I do not know. But surely this is a most improper argument to advance if we are concerned with the ethical considerations of the act itself. I do not think that T.S. would approve of the act if it were to have taken place at a time nicely calculated to win sympathy for the coloured people's cause. To kill a man because it is a cute propaganda dodge is to me an abominable thing to do, but I do not think Pratt's ineffective attempt can be considered in this category.

Again, it may have been utterly impolitic for the Editors of

FREEDOM to have published the article they did at the time they did, for reasons T.S. and others have mentioned - I do not know. But the fact that they did reflects entirely to their credit, and I think it more important that FREEDOM should retain its record of honesty than that it should seek to capture more readers on a short-term basis.

Correspondence

● *Ernie Crosswell*

Dear Editors,

Apropos the attempt on Verwoerd's life, it would seem that our editors, having grown out of the bomb-throwing stage themselves, are taking a most questionable, barbaric delight in watching someone else do their dirty work for them.

I myself have grown out of the *absolute* pacifist position but I certainly cannot imagine that killing Verwoerd would guarantee the slightest progress.

Surely the rational approach to David Pratt's action should be: 'Verwoerd had it coming to him: some poor desperate devil was bound to try it sooner or later'. It was understandable but hardly praiseworthy.

Ernie Crosswell

Slough

● *Louis Billerey*

Comrades,

You have justified David Pratt's action as a generous gesture. In the absence of any definition of the word in your editorial of

30.4.60, I have taken you to mean that given in the Concise Oxford Dictionary, which gives 'gesture' as a 'step or move calculated to evoke response from another or to convey (especially friendly) intentions'.

We can dismiss the idea that David Pratt wished to convey friendly intentions, let us assume he wished to convey unfriendly ones. This could have significance only if he had other intentions than killing Verwoerd, and was shooting to miss, or at any rate not to kill. The fact that he shot for the head does not show that in fact he was doing this.

As for responses, there are a variety which David Pratt may have evoked. To show 'that there are whites whose sense of justice transcends considerations of race or class' is indeed most important.

There is at least one other aspect however, as FREEDOM puts it, 'it has given the ruling clique in South Africa a feeling of insecurity'. True, but the usual response to fear in rulers of Verwoerd's ilk is an increase in their intransigence which 'fosters a similar intransigence among black Africans', leading, of course to more fear among the Verwoerds, and re-doubled oppression. The result of this response so far as I can see is more inter-racial hatred, and thus the negation of David Pratt's good work in showing that some South African whites are anti-racial.

In the absence of any evidence one way or the other about this however, and although emotionally I am all on David Pratt's side for his good intentions, I have my doubts as to the actual results of his actions.

There remains the time-honoured question for critics of particular actions: 'What would you have done?' If I had David Pratt's opportunity I would have subjected Verwoerd to some kind of indignity, like slapping a jelly in his face, as happened to Mosley this week. If enough people did that kind of thing often enough, politicians would become the laughing stock they deserve to be. That may be a pious hope, but laughter can be a powerful weapon, as any demagogue can attest.

Yours fraternally,

Louis Billerey

London, April 29

● *Albert McCarthy*

Dear Friends,

Congratulations on the original 'Too Bad He Missed' and 'In Defence of David Pratt'. The reaction of the left wingers and pacifists to David Pratt's courageous action is so typical that it almost amounts to parody.

Your correspondent T.S., when he wonders how some anarchists 'reconcile individual freedom with assassination', would appear to subscribe to the idea that one should not interfere with the 'individual freedom' of a tyrant to oppress one. This is surely turning the concept of individual freedom on its head!

Pratt's action was certainly the result of desperation and one is not naive enough to believe that the exit of Verwoerd would mean the end of apartheid, but it at least might result in some of his followers hesitating before plunging any further into tyranny. T.S. claims that: 'It is a mistake to assume that by eliminating individuals we can improve a situation ...' As a generalisation this may be true but it is not applicable in every circumstance. As a concrete example, it would be rash to assume that the removal of Franco would make no difference at all. When a régime is as internally rotten as Franco's the exit of the figurehead might well result in the collapse of a whole structure.

Sincerely,

Albert J. McCarthy

St Ives, May 1

● *Laurens Otter*

Comrade,

I did not write before about the Verwoerd article because I spent most of last week in Great Wakering preparing for the first Foulness action and had not time; and when I returned hearing that T.S. had written I considered there was no need to write further knowing that most of your readers will agree with him. I was saved the embarrassment of having to defend FREEDOM by the fact that for most of the March I was carrying (or reviving after carrying) the PPU banner; and so such as I sold were in fact chiefly to friends of mine who know my views on the subject.

If as you admit in your first article that the assassination of Verwoerd will not remove the basic problems that divide the people of South Africa, it is plainly stupid to suppose that his removal is going to produce a better in his place. You have only to look at the assassination of Bandaranaike to see this; there might well have been some case for your argument if Verwoerd, like some South American dictators had had no body of opinion or influential strata behind him; there might even have been an arguable case for the Nihilist tactic of sending him a warning before that unless he amended his rule he would be assassinated (this was a method that in its early days did achieve positive results, but the Nihilist groups became authoritarian cliques, and as Tolstoy shows they became interested only in Power themselves.). You have argued too often that tyranny is the inevitable product of Government and Privilege now to turn round and say that the removal of one tryant can achieve anything; the short-term effects so far seen are that whereas a substantial body of the Nationalist Party was becoming 'revisionist' and advocating the amelioration of Apartheid; it has now been routed by the extremists. The South African Government has been able to divert World interest from Sharpeville to the attentat and in so doing to pretend in some twisted way that Sharpeville was necessary, and that wonderful burst of world-wide protest that we saw last month has been killed.

Unlike T.S. and others who may write to you on this subject, my Pacifism is purely a question of expediency, I do not believe that a Free Society can be brought about by violence or even that any substantial amelioration can be so brought about, and I believe that generally speaking violence gives tyrants the excuse they want; so I shall not attempt to answer your 'reply' except to point out that there is record of some mental aberration in David Pratt, who two years ago was refused permission to land in Holland after he had announced that the purpose of his visit was to shoot his wife; while not asking all FREEDOM readers to agree that shooting wives is an act of insanity, I would suggest that announcing this to the Customs shows a certain lack of balance.

I can only conclude by saying that the lack of scientific analysis in your article was such that it might push people in reaction to the desperate step of joining the SPGB, not as Tony fears of having a go at Macmillan.
Yours fraternally,
L. Otter

London

● *A.R. Lacey*

Dear Editors,
   I am sorry to be one of those whom sheer laziness prevented from writing about Pratt. I cannot rake up much indignation at Pratt or sympathy for Verwoerd, or for those who reserve moral horror for the killing of oppressors and mild regrets for the killing of victims. But to say this (which needs saying) is not to condone or advocate political assassination.
   T.S. asks whether those who think Macmillan is leading the country to disaster should kill him, and you do not answer. No doubt one can recall the Hitler plot of 1944, which few would disapprove of. But where are we to draw the line? For one like myself, who is not a complete pacifist, the question is difficult; I had thought modern anarchism was pacifist, but if not, then surely you must face the question too. Perhaps we can make a start like this: Bloodshed in South Africa, horrible though it is, has been small and sporadic (think of the Stalin purges, the India-Pakistan dispute, or modern China).The attempt on Hitler, whatever its result, could hardly have added significantly to the violence already raging.
   But in South Africa, however much oppression there may be, the deluge has not come, and may not come; but Pratt's action is just the sort of thing that could spark it off. You defend him by reference to the right of self-defence; but Pratt couldn't possibly have relied on this. No-one was committing violence on him personally, and Verwoerd wasn't personally committing it on anyone. But if you start extending the right, remember that the pro-H-bomb types do just the same. I do not wish to be hypocriti-

cal about this; my own first reaction to Verwoerd's being shot was 'serve him right!' But a considered moral judgement need not be the same as an immediate emotional reaction. If FREEDOM is to depart so far from the image of anarchism built up in many people's minds, you should surely give us a far more thorough examination of the problem than this week's article, which only reaches the main topic at all right at the end, and then agrees that violence breeds violence.

I hope the laziness of readers like myself won't make you think we should not be interested in a thorough discussion of the whole problem of when, if ever, an anarchist or sympathiser can approve of violent action.

Fraternally yours,
A.R. Lacey

Birmingham, May 3

● *Arlo Tatum*

Dear Editor,

David Pratt is a sick man, and has been institutionalised for psychiatric treatment several times. Your hero-worship is based on ignorance.[1] On 11th April he appeared in Johannesburg court, and this was reported in South African papers. He therefore no longer is being held under the emergency regulations.[2]

I agree that his action should not be ignored, but both FREEDOM and *Peace News* often 'ignore' items of interest when they are well covered by the regular press, and there is some justification for it from a space point of view. Certainly it is neither cowardly nor dishonest. *Peace News*, heaven knows, is vulnerable enough to attack without your having to invent anything.[3]

And what of the last two paragraphs? Are you saying that Pratt was acting in self-defence, or that Verwoerd should have exercised his right of self-defence more effectively? Was this irrelevance an effort to start an argument with your pacifist readers? If so, you will delight us pacifists, but probably more the non-pacifists who have heard it all before.[4]

As one of those who did not protest the first article on David Pratt, please accept my apology. I had assumed it was contributed by a doddering old anarchist who had failed to keep up with the times, but nonetheless was remembering FREEDOM in his will. I now see that some anarchists - as well as some pacifists - seriously think they can lead our movements backwards.

Sincerely

Arlo Tatum

London, May 2

Editor's Footnotes to Arlo Tatum's letter

Arlo Tatum's letter is one of the shortest 'protest' letters we have received, yet apart from the last paragraph which is too childish to be taken seriously, there is not a single sentence in it which could not be challenged! To save space we have commented in the form of footnotes to his letter.

1. We have always attacked the cult of personalities so there is no question of 'hero-worship' when we defend David Pratt, Caryl Chessman or Sacco and Vanzetti. We ignore the motives behind David Pratt's attentat and may one day be proved wrong in attributing the generous motives to his act which we have done; we may of course also be proved right. Whatever the final verdict, we prefer to be proved wrong than to have remained silent until our silence was proved to be wrong! Tatum dismisses David Pratt by saying he is a mentally sick man. Would his attitude to the attentat have been different if he had not thought David Pratt a sick man?

2. We should be interested to see reports from the South African paper to which Tatum refers. Meantime we will quote to him the *Reuter* report from Cape Town April 11 (printed in *The Times* the following day): \

David Pratt, the farmer alleged to have shot Dr. Verwoerd, the South African Prime Minister, on Saturday, is not to be tried at present but is detained under the emergency regulations - and may not even be mentioned by name in future. An announcement to-night to this effect followed a day of suspense at the Johannesburg magistrates' court, where he was due to appear, and long consultations between detectives and legal authorities.

3. To explain away *Peace News*' silence on the grounds that both they and FREEDOM 'often ignore items of interest when they

are well covered by the regular press ...' is a pretty lame excuse. We were not expecting a report but a comment. The 'regular Press' with the exception of the *Observer* deplored the act as was to be expected. And as we showed the so-called 'radical' press chose to ignore it rather than to have either to join the chorus of shocked Fleet Street editorial writers or to commit themselves to trying to understand and explain the act in the context of the present situation in South Africa. We imagine that the editors concerned felt that to express regrets for Verwoerd would be hypocritical, and so they said nothing (a similar line to that adopted by Great Britain at the United Nations debate on South Africa when it 'abstained' from voting. The Fleet Street press hailed this as a step forward, the 'radicals' roundly condemned it!) If Mr. Tatum will look up *Peace News* for April 15 he will see on page 9 a report from that paper's Johannesburg correspondent. It says very little that the daily press here did not say about news censorship in South Africa. In view of *P.N.*'s silence on the David Pratt attentat, the headline 'News Blackout Keeps South Africans in the Dark' makes curious reading!

4. We assume that our readers are people who have the necessary feelings and imagination to be able to identify themselves with a cause or a struggle whether or not they are personally directly involved. Surely we are able to identify ourselves with the black South Africans in their struggle against the pass system and their status of inferiority in relation to the white South Africans without having to be dark skinned? Only someone apparently as thick skinned as Mr. Tatum could consider our last two paragraphs 'irrelevant'. What we are saying, Mr. Tatum, was that David Pratt's action was inspired by the horrors of the Sharpeville massacre, and the policy of apartheid; that in identifying himself with the victims of Verwoerd's policies he was acting in self-defence. As to recognising Verwoerd's right of self-defence too, well of course we do. From his point of view it was too bad that his permanent body-guard was temporarily off his guard!

● *Tony Smythe*

Comrades,

When FREEDOM takes five columns, or one page, in two weeks to deal with a recent, universally reported incident, we can safely assume that the editors are gunning for someone or something. This week the National Press (honourable exception, the *Observer*), the minority weeklies and poor old *Peace News* are treated collectively to a pop-gun bombardment. So too are the cowardly (?) left wing and those muddled pacifists, patted on the head one minute and kicked on the arse the next. The gunmen must now be gloating over the intended carnage, so universally administered that non-violent fellow anarchists were expected to perish with the rest.

Too bad you missed. Take off your dark glasses, you cannot see a thing with them on; shave round your ears, things have been happening lately; stop buying weapons from Woolworths toy counters, this is a nuclear age.

What was this marathon squeal all about? Can it be in the midst of these dead sea scrolls we can find a practical policy or some moral principle at stake? No. In constructive thinking they are as barren as Trafalgar Square on May Day. Instead it seems that some (I hope not many) comrades have found a Messiah, a new patron saint (was the old one Jack the Ripper?), a symbol for the future. I fully expect next week to be asked for a contribution towards the David Pratt Memorial Fund and next time I venture, I might say with caution, into the Bookshop his bust will leer across at me from the counter.

In a fine display of conjectural gymnastics we are assured that this paragon of anarchist virtue has a conscience which prevents him from rationalising his privileged status. Yes comrades, he is a member of the upper crust who came over to our side, a reformed character destined to save the movement from apathy and the PPU.

Some of us might protest however that this 170lbs. of angelic benevolence is a pistol-packing lunatic and that his motives for any particular action are known only to himself and his psychoanalyst. What do we know about him in addition to the information grudgingly offered last week? He caught religion lately and studies yoga, a bad sign. He was thrown out of Holland for pulling a gun on his wife, a minor offence, and has been under treatment at various mental institutions for short periods, probably doing it for kicks. We know more than this, for instance he was brilliant at school, but I have merely selected one or two of the more reassuring aspects of his noble character. However all this is beside the point. Normal or insane, why in heavens name must we be treated to one whole page of the hero treatment? It is fortunate that *Peace News* left the affair out, although I cannot imagine it was for policy reasons, for this at least could help me to get it into perspective again. Has FREEDOM ever been so corny? 'We refuse to let the self-named "direct actionists" pass by David Pratt.' 'Sharpeville needed a David Pratt to save the dignity of mankind.' The last sentence is almost reminiscent of Calvary.

I pointed out in my last letter that one could have sympathy for him whilst deploring his act, I never anticipated that by the next edition my sympathy and FREEDOM's admiration would have been translated into frenzied worship. Forgive me therefore if I appear to be somewhat less than charitable to Mr. Pratt this time.

His admirer, the marksman, not only missed, the shots went so wide that I cannot imagine what the target had originally been. A few practical words on the tangible results of the assassination attempt or even an objective discussion on the practice of assassination no matter how out-of-date it might have been would have reassured us that FREEDOM could remain constructive even during an intellectual blackout.

The last section on non-violence was I think more important and I will try and deal with it briefly. Non-violent resistance is a tactic or method the underlying principle of which is a respect for human life as being sacrosanct. It is true that in general terms one's own life is equally as sacrosanct as the next person's but it is equally true that if it comes to a choice between the life of one committed to non-violence and one who is not, the commitment could and should still prevent the use of violence on the part of the defender. This does not take into account such factors as avoiding the homicidal type, a useful defence mechanism which most of us practice, also by a non-violent attitude and reasoned argument dissuading the attacker or if this fails beating it at top speed. The case of David Pratt was however not one of self defence, he was not protecting himself from Verwoerd, rather it was he who was doing the attacking. Therefore this has nothing to do with the individual's right to defend himself. The question for South Africa is what is the most effective method of overcoming oppression. The truism was admitted that violence breeds violence and therefore presumably the editors share my view that non-violent resistance is the only course open to the Africans. If they are going to make exceptions for imaginary cases of self-defence, they are merely using the same arguments which we are accustomed to hear from our power politicians. No country has an attacking force, only a system of defence. This does not prevent other nations from being attacked.

Fraternally,
T.S.

London, May 2

● *Hugh Brock* (*Editor Peace News*)

Dear Comrade Editor,

Re your charge that *Peace News* was guilty of being cowardly and dishonest in not writing about Verwoerd's assailant. Our Johannesburg correspondent Basil Delaine - reputed to be one of the few white professional journalists the Africans trust - did file a story on David Pratt. It unfortunately reached us after our Aldermaston March issue had gone to press, and we did not consider it sufficiently topical to run the following week when new dispatches were arriving from Johannesburg.

That is all there is to it. An error of judgement on our part not to have run the despatch the following week in an eight page issue already crowded with news of Aldermaston and other African material? Perhaps yes, but surely not an occasion for the use of the words cowardly and dishonest.

Of our two South African correspondents, one, Basil Delaine, was writing his dispatch in a building which angry Nationalists had threatened to dynamite; the other, Patrick Duncan, was out in the streets endeavouring to use his influence and authority as the son of a former Governor-General to stop police brutalities.

At home in the past eighteen months some eight or nine of our staff and voluntary workers have gone to jail because of their opposition to all violence.

Surely our failure to denounce the activities of one neurotic gunman does not warrant such sweeping charges.

Yours sincerely,

Hugh Brock,

London, May 12.

● *Nicolas Walter*

If there is to be a counting of heads in the dispute between David Pratt and FREEDOM versus the pacifists and others, I should like to be reckoned as a supporter of anyone who has the guts to shoot a tyrant, whatever his motives and whatever the possible consequences.

N.W.

London, May 13.

[There is no question, so far as we are concerned, of counting heads, though we appreciate our friend's communication. FREEDOM exists, and we 'argue' in its columns, because we want people to use their heads. - Editor]

● *Milward Casey*

Dear Comrades,

The second article printed in FREEDOM on the defence of David Pratt has succeeded in goading me to write the letter which should have been written on reading the first. Like you my first remark was one of satisfaction - 'about time too' - I think it was. It seems I was also guilty of a heresy in feeling relief that Pratt was white not black.

I must admit I get no feeling of elation from the idea that a mighty massacre may unite the liberals of the world who would rise and swamp apartheid.

This feeling of relief I speak of I remember having in Burma on hearing of the dropping of the first atomic bomb. My doubts began a few days later on hearing of the effect and what it meant, the relief turned to horror which has grown ever since. So with this shooting, a day or so of relief then the doubts becoming overwhelming on seeing the actual thing on television. I must repeat what T.S. says in his letter, that we spare pity on the sight of a man shot through the face, obviously in great pain, his head being nursed in his wife's hands.

A great many words have been written in these two articles but this film has either not been seen or has been deliberately ignored. Films of the Sharpeville shootings have also been shown but I must say that my revulsion at violence done to a human being is no way altered by the victim's colour or what he may have done. Even so, my pity and sympathy are with David Pratt. He has suffered and will suffer for an act I and most readers of FREEDOM have not the guts to commit - even if we wished.

It has convinced me more than ever that non-violent resistance though less satisfyingly dramatic, is the only method that should be used. But although it may sound contradictory, I believe I would kill to save my own life and that of my wife and child. On the other hand I would not commit an act for any moral or ethical belief or any society for which it would mean the sacrifice of our lives.

This letter may seem emotional and sentimental but it is deliberate, I refuse to intellectualise them out of existence.

Yours sincerely,
Milward Casey.

Newport, May 5

● *Norman Day*

Dear Editorial Committee

It was, perhaps, not politic to have applauded David Pratt's attempted assassination of Verwoerd, but since when have Anarchists been politicians? In any case, even if the article 'Too Bad He Missed' did alienate a few mild revolutionaries about to be converted to anarchism and embarrassed their potential converters, it eased the embarrassment of those of us who had in vain looked elsewhere for an expression of the general consensus of opinion on the subject in order to prove to South African friends in this country that not all our papers think the shooting of one white more heinous than the killing of 91 blacks. To correct the impression the remainder of that issue seemingly gave - mistakenly, I trust - that anarchism is 'respectable' and for ever turning the other cheek, was also something worth doing.

Inference that the country as a whole endorsed the horror expressed by Macmillan and practically every newspaper editorial, and that those who pray prayed for Verwoerd's speedy recovery and consequent return to brutality is inference, I would suggest, that those who criticised the article are out of touch with reality. The CND, though, has always been thus. Fondly they imagine that those who march with them and support them are as pacifist as they are, conveniently ignoring, for example, the Hungary-stained Communist Party banners sprouting in their midst. The Communists, it may be argued, are in a minority, the bulk of support being drawn from the Labour Party. Despite their presence on the march, though, Hugh Gaitskell was still able two weeks later to confidently predict that the Labour Party is not 'going pacifist'. People who unless they get married or buried in the interim will not go near a minister of religion until they march again next Easter consent to receiving Canon Collins' blessing in Trafalgar Square, so does that make them pillars of the church as well?

The leadership and active membership of CND is a 'Popular Front' of religious, political and Trade Union dissenters, dissenting because conformity has not given them the 'fruits of office' to which they think they are entitled. Each is anxious that the rank and file be moulded into his own image and made to serve a purpose to which disarmament is subsidiary, what they cannot understand being the opposition of the rank and file to nuclear warfare on the very personal basis of a desire to continue living rather than on political or theological grounds.

Similarly, those who suffer because of Verwoerd and his like are not concerned to discuss ethics but wish to be rid of him because of what he has done to them and what he will do. That country's industrialists are now intriguing to free themselves if not of Verwoerd of the economic consequences of apartheid and a seemingly perpetual state of emergency, but having nothing to freely offer or withdraw neither the Africans or David Pratt who acted on their behalf were or are in a position to bargain. Less even than is ours, their labour is not their own, it being the police and the pass system that makes wage-slaves of them. Not hunger, but police in Saracens break strikes, so what is the African and those who support him to do? Violence, it is true, breeds violence, but in South Africa, and not only in South Africa, non-violence also breeds it.

There is no one blue-print of society, therefore no one course of action. As it is claimed to have done in India, non-violence can attain its ends only if there is a third party as final arbiter to which the oppressed can appeal. British troops firing on protesting Indians resulted in questions being asked by whichever party was in opposition and letters being written to the press, the officer concerned being sacrificed as a consequence and sometimes the minister, too. Indian troops firing on Indians, however, is merely a news item and evidence of what happens when independence is granted, so that non-violence has had to be discarded in favour of something *à la* Kashmir. In Germany, the Jews had no one to whom to appeal to see fair play and did not themselves organise in their own defence, so almost to a man were exterminated. Possibly, both when they were rounded up and when they entered the gas chamber, Jews non-violently protested. By then it was too late.

The moment he was in power it was too late to non-violently protest against Syngman Rhee, so would it have been preferable had there been no violent protests a few weeks ago and the ageing dictator allowed to remain in power until he died of natural causes? One hundred and seventy-two people died during that brief revolt, but how many died during his fifteen years of office? Unless they are forcibly deposed or die violently, dictators live to a ripe old age, Stalin, Salazar, Petain, de Gaulle and Adenauer joining with Syngman Rhee in proof that theirs is a long-lived profession. Killing them is an extreme form of protest that does not necessarily change anything, but if the lives of their subjects are not sacred, neither is theirs. Amongst leaders, of course, leaders are sacrosanct, but the led do not always think so.

Tactics and morals are inextricably mixed: a plea to morality being a tactical measure, a refusal to do anything generally held to be 'immoral' good public relations. If, though, it is thought they are separate and a difference in degree in no way constitutes a difference in kind, there is no answer, only a question. If alone in a room with a beer- or power-drunk individual about to press a button unleashing nuclear warfare on the world, exhortations having failed do we resign ourselves to the fact that if he doesn't press the button someone else will, or do we violently protest with the heaviest paper-weight to hand?

Fraternally,
Norman Day

London, May 2

Editorial

Had we been in T.S.'s confidence we would have advised him not to submit his letter for publication, on the grounds that anyone not knowing the writer might conclude that he was a little *exalté*, and since one of his strongest arguments against David Pratt was that he is 'a pistol-packing lunatic' he would surely have argued his case more convincingly had he calmly, factually and pacifically demolished our arguments. Not only does he not do this, but he even invents 'facts' such as, for example, that 'he [Pratt] was thrown out of Holland for pulling a gun on his wife'. The only story we have read which resembles this one is that David Pratt was *refused admission* to Holland because when asked the routine question put to all foreigners entering Holland, 'what was his business in coming to Holland' he replied that he was coming to shoot his wife. T.S. to strengthen his argument, presumably, needs to add a few damaging embellishments. Obviously the original story, if true, is hardly convincing. What man set on killing his wife would be so foolish as to tell an Immigration Officer, of all people? It will not have escaped T.S.'s eagle eye that when David Pratt attempted to kill Verwoerd he neither called at the local police station or advised Verwoerd of his intention before the event.

T.S. also tells us that David Pratt 'caught religion lately and studies yoga, a bad sign'. Of what? *Peace News* which published an enlarged edition last week as 'part of our contribution to a new drive for Christian action in the cause of world peace' should be informed at once!

The accusation of 'hero-treatment', 'frenzied worship' in the way we have dealt with the David Pratt case does not stand up to examination. As we pointed out to Arlo Tatum last week when he referred to 'hero-worship', we have always combated the cult of personalities and leaders, which is more than can be said either of *Peace News* or the minority 'Left' Press. We dealt with the *attentat*, in the first place, because no revolutionary paper, nor any paper concerned with the South African struggle could surely *ignore* it. And as we stated in our first article we approved of the act and only regretted that it had not been successful. A point of view which many people, including some anarchists, do not share with us. Our columns have been open to receive the disagreements with our defence of David Pratt. The second article - of this - according to T.S. - 'marathon squeal' was to our minds fully justified, *irrespective of whether one agreed or not with* FREE-DOM's *'line'* in view of the cowardly - yes, cowardly! - conspiracy of silence among the minority journals.

It was justified firstly because we could not accept that the significance of David Pratt's action should be passed over, a mere news item among the daily crop, which is forgotten before it is understood. Since we approved of his act this was the least it should have inspired us to do.* When we also found that we were in fact alone, in this country at least, in trying to explain his action, then there was even more reason to raise our voices in his defence and to provoke those who condemned him by their silence, to speak up.

The second letter we print on this page comes from Hugh Brock, editor of *Peace News*. It is true that we have not succeeded in provoking Mr. Brock to discuss the David Pratt case in *Peace News*; nor have we succeeded in persuading him to have second thoughts about this example of direct action in South Africa. Or should it be *first* thoughts? For if we are to believe what he writes - and he assures us that 'that is all there is to it' - then it would seem that Mr. Brock has given the matter very little thought indeed.

He admits that *P.N.*'s Johannesburg correspondent had 'filed a story' which 'unfortunately' reached the paper too late for the 15th April issue 'and we did not consider it sufficiently topical to run the following week when new dispatches were arriving from Johannesburg'. This all sounds very important until one refers to the issue for April 22. What happened to the 'new dispatches' from Johannesburg? We reproduce them in full, headlines in-cluded:

---

*   The pacifists surely will understand this attitude. We see from *P.N.* (May 13) that a Committee has been started for those arrested at Foulness and now serving prison sentences, for the purposes of helping prisoners and dependents and 'to publicise the reasons for the former's non-violent action at Foulness'.

Families starving in S. Africa

from Basil Delaine, Johannesburg

Reports smuggled from Cato Manor, Durban, allege that many families are starving.

Reports likewise from Langa location, Cape Town, allege that there is typhoid in the location.

Is or has the water been cut off?

IN LONDON a spokesman at South Africa House dismissed these reports as 'quite absurd'.

[And what was 'the other African material' in this 'already crowded issue'? A whole-page plus half a column for a speech by Dr. Nkrumah to a 'Positive Action Conference for Peace and Security in Africa' delivered in Accra on April 7 which was illustrated by the smiling portrait of the Leader (hero-worship indeed!) and headlined: 'We are devoted to non-violent action - Prime Minister Nkrumah'. Columns of political platitudes with an occasional appeal to 'positive non-violent action'. But in vain did we search for any statement by the Premier that he had taken the first step by abolishing his police force, his army and his navy, modest though they may be compared with those of the Big Powers. In vain did we search the editorial columns of *P.N.* for a sobering comment to the smooth words of this wiliest of South African politicians!]

In the third paragraph of his letter, Hugh Brock informs FREE-DOM readers that *Peace News* has two influential correspondents in South Africa and we can only rejoice at his good fortune, but regret that he should have so little space for their dispatches. Would he be agreeable to letting FREEDOM have Basil Delaine's story on David Pratt which we would undertake to print whether it is favourable or unfavourable to our particular point of view?

In the fourth paragraph of his letter Mr. Brock gives us the jail records of *P.N.* staff during the past 18 months as proof, we presume, that *P.N.* was neither cowardly nor dishonest in not dealing with the David Prat attentat. For in the fifth paragraph he writes: 'Surely our failure to *denounce* the activities of one *neurotic gunman* does not warrant such sweeping charges' (our italics).

So David Pratt is a 'neurotic gunman'. The three part question
we would first put to Hugh Brock is: Would your opinion of his act
be modified if you were convinced that he was not 'neurotic'? If
so, why? If not, why gratuitously refer to him as a *neurotic*
gunman?

The second question is: Why the use of the pejorative term
'gunman' to describe David Pratt? The Oxford Concise Dictionary confirms our concept of the word as pejorative when it defines
gunman as '(esp., U.S. sl) armed robber'. Is this a fair description
of David Pratt?

The pacifists pride themselves on their tolerance and understanding of human weaknesses and failings, which they seek to
overcome by example. Mr. Brock and his friends it would appear
have all the time in the world to encourage people to learn how to
be arrested, and in South Africa, to be shot down in cold blood if
need be, in order to seek to teach the Verwoerds of this world to
mend their ways. But when an individual (and no one has said that
David Pratt had been involved in South African politics) tries to
strike down the tyrant, they haven't a word to spare not even more
in sorrow than in anger! When provoked to say something, well ...
there it is for all to see elsewhere on this page. A 'neurotic
gunman' who, if they had written anything about him in their
paper, would have been 'denounced'.

The integral pacifist is to our minds as unfree as the individual
who knows no alternative to violence in regulating his relations
with his fellow beings.

Because we supported the view that 'violence breeds violence',
our critic T.S. jumped to the conclusion that we shared his view
that 'nonviolent resistance is the only course open to the Africans'
and then (if readers will refer to the last paragraph of his letter), he
equates self-defence of the African with the self-defence referred
to by Khrushchev, Eisenhower and the lesser power politicians.

We do not accept that self-defence by a people against its
government or a section of the community which maintains its
power and privileges by a naked display of force, has any affinity
with the 'self-defence' to which the political leaders are always
referring in justification of massive armaments programmes.

And we do not accept our correspondent's assumption that the
only course open to the Africans in South Africa is non-violent

resistance. Nor, on the other hand, do we believe that violence is the only course open to them. Verwoerd and his Apartheiders can only be overthrown when the power of the Africans is greater than his power. It is obviously not a question of numbers, for if it were, black Africa would never have been enslaved by the white man in the first place. It is not a question of superior armaments, or Algeria should long ago have succumbed to rule by the French settlers and Kenya would not be in sight of independence (from white rule, not from politicians!) in spite of the military defeat of Mau Mau. Similarly in the cases of Palestine and now Cyprus.

'Violence breeds violence' is a 'truism' declares T.S. But in fact it is not, for violence as well as breeding violence has also resulted in the growth and development of non-violent movements. And it has done so because there are those who have convincingly expounded the view that non-violence is a more effective reply to violence. We believe that the social revolution, as we understand it, will be achieved non-violently, because the success of such a revolution depends on a majority of the people wanting it above all else - which means knowing what they want. The success of non-violent resistance depends on numbers and knowledge and this is *power* which not even the machine guns of the privileged minority can overcome. When the people are so strong, they have no need to *initiate* violence. When they do, it is a clear indication of their weakness.

But when on the one hand they have not the informed support to overthrow the tyrant yet nevertheless seek to curb his excesses, as say in South Africa, is counter-violence such an ineffective weapon? And to those who say it is, we ask what more effective alternative is at hand?

May 21, 1960

Correspondence

● *John Pilgrim*

Dear Sir,

Once again I see that FREEDOM has successfully set out to alienate some of its newer readers. This time by a cheap jibe against people who demonstrated outside South Africa House in the week following the Sharpeville massacre. Had there been no protest FREEDOM would presumably, and quite rightly, have attacked the terrible apathy that could let such crimes happen without a murmur of objection. But there was a protest and a large and prolonged one at that, which FREEDOM loftily dismisses as 'Pacifists, New Leftists, Communists and Socialists (no anarchists I notice) making a mild nuisance of themselves, as far as the British authorities were concerned'.

(Just for the record there were also anarchists, conservatives, and people so apolitical they wouldn't even buy FREEDOM.)

Yet in fact the demonstration was of far greater significance than the armchair anarchist who wrote the rather silly statement quoted above seems to realise. In the first place a considerable amount of money was collected from sympathetic passers-by, money which was desperately needed by the dependants and relatives of those killed, wounded or imprisoned, and who have no means of help apart from what we choose to send them.

Again, apart from the minor point that the demonstration helped to show the depth of revulsion that we felt, to the authorities in South Africa House, the demonstrations were widely reported abroad and did a great deal to compensate for the British attitude in the Security Council.

But the most important aspect of the demonstrations in the week following Sharpeville has been expressed by Ronald Segal, Tennyson Makiwane and numerous white South Africans who joined us in picketing. 'You have no idea', they said, 'how heartening this is to those of us who are trying to fight apartheid from within the Union. Demonstrations in Britain have a value out of all proportion to their size, their effect in the Union is without any doubt much greater than any of you in this country realise.' So perhaps after all, we were doing more than make 'a mild nuisance' of ourselves to the British authorities.

The same article later goes on to say that the regrettably unsuccessful attempt to assassinate Dr. Verwoerd left us paralysed and speechless. Did it indeed. If we were paralysed and speechless, I am at a loss to find terms to apply to the writer of this article, to whom all action and none appears to be equally reprehensible.

In fact there has been a considerable amount of action going on with the twin purpose of raising funds and demonstrating our disapproval. A Direct Action Committee has been formed, to urge industrial action in the docks and distributive centres. Two young men have arranged a jazz and folk music concert (May 10th, St. Pancras Town Hall) and engaged some of the biggest names in this country to attend. The 'Music Against Apartheid' Committee have been busy recording an L.P. of folk music to be issued on their own label 'Music AA', Josh White heading their list of singers. The African families who receive aid as a result of these activities, I feel, will not be so contemptuous as the writer of your leading article. All over the country hundreds of actionist groups are springing up and I invite the nameless writer of your leading article, when he has finished upsetting the new readers that FREEDOM has won recently, to come out from behind his anonymous columns and do something himself.

We know we can't have a free society tomorrow, we know that our efforts may result in Black Fascism replacing White Fascism, we don't think that the struggle for freedom in Africa will end with the establishment of a Pan African Republic, but we do feel that we should do anything and everything to help those living under Verwoerd's tyranny today.

Incidentally, I went along to South Africa House to make an individual anarchist protest, that I as an anarchist felt should be made, as loudly and as often as possible. I found a lot of people sympathetic to our ideas. How many of them have now been lost because of last week's snivelling attack I do not know. To me anarchism means responsibility not the sort of indiscriminate needling that was shown in last week's article (the sort of sensationalism FREEDOM always condemns in the capitalist press) done to provoke reader reaction. Any South African fighting against apartheid will tell those of you who are in doubt, that any action, any demonstration, is valuable.

As for myself, I am an anarchist because I believe in bettering the human condition (yes, my own included), not because I want to sit back and say to the wounded, the dying and the starving, in Africa, in Korea and Turkey, 'What can you expect, you've a government'. It's true we won't get a free society by demonstrations in Trafalgar Square - but we won't get one by ignoring human suffering either.
John Pilgrim

London, May 1960

● *P. Britten, S.E.Parker*

Dear Comrades,

We agree with A.R. Lacey on the need for a 'thorough examination' of the problems raised by the attentat of David Pratt. Such acts as these have always produced varying and often conflicting reactions amongst anarchists and it is doubtful if complete accord is possible regarding the attitude to be adopted towards them. It is certain, however, that the name-calling and irrelevancies which have marred the present controversy are of no help, in reaching an understanding of the difference of opinion expressed. The space which they take up could be more fruitfully occupied with serious and relevant comment.

It seems to us that to argue, as did the writer of 'Too Bad He Missed', that assassination 'is the only language that dictators and tyrants understand' is too slick and facile. Like Ernie Crosswell we are no longer absolute pacifists and we can conceive of some situations in which we would be prepared to use violence in defence of our persons. Violence in itself, however, is not a means of creating understanding. FREEDOM has often pointed out that the use of violence in the shape of prisons and police is useless when dealing with the problem of 'ordinary' delinquency. Surely the same applies to the problem of delinquents who wield political power? An attentat may result in a temporary relaxation of a repressive policy, as was sometimes the case in Czarist Russia, but such a relaxation arises from fear rather than from understanding. However effective fear may prove as a short-term 'deterrent', it is useless as a fundamental contribution towards abolishing tyranny.

On the other hand, the kind of blanket condemnation of assassinations in which pacifists tend to indulge is simply an inversion of that attitude which sees in violence a sovereign remedy for social wrongs. Non-violent direct action can be a good tactic, but it is not a panacea and its advocates should refrain from insisting that others accept it as the only way to combat oppression.
Yours fraternally,
P. Britten,
S.E. Parker

Bristol, May 13, 1960

● *Arthur W. Uloth*

Dear Comrades,

I do not approve of the use of violence which seems to be self-defeating in the struggle for freedom, but I am glad that you had the courage to publish the David Pratt article. After all, it is what lots of people thought, but did not care to commit to print. However much one may be against violence, it is difficult to feel genuinely distressed about men like Verwoerd, and 'A Pity He (David Pratt) Missed' would sum up the views of most people I talked to about it.

The danger of political assassination lies of course in the principle being extended. If one goes on from shooting the dictator to shooting the enemies of freedom in general. Many people no doubt supported the Second World War, despite their strong feelings against violence, because they could think of no other way of stopping the Nazis. Yet from fighting against Nazism they were led to the inexorable logic of events to waging a war against the German people themselves, to busting dams and drowning large numbers, to bombing cities and roasting the citizens alive in their cellars, to the final atrocity against the Japanese cities from which people are still dying today. In other words, by fighting the Nazis and their allies they became temporary Nazis themselves, and I think that to fight tyranny by tyranny's weapons will always lead one to becoming very like the thing one is fighting against.

Therefore, while I think it is very good that Freedom should speak up for David Pratt, I do not think he should be regarded as someone to be emulated. The disappearance of Verwoerd from the scene would probably make little difference. As far as the man himself is concerned the *attentat* has probably strengthened him in his views. Supposing Freedom Bookshop was wrecked by Mosleyite hooligans, wouldn't that make the editors of Freedom more determined than ever to carry on?

The problem of self-defence is of course a thorny one. Mankind, in all its history, has never really found any answer to the problem of tyranny. How is one to resist such a régime as that of the Nazis or the South African Nationalists without resort to war? I simply do not know. Non-violent resistance requires more courage than armed struggle, perhaps too much courage for most people. But it seems the only hope.

Yours fraternally,

Arthur W. Uloth

Alfriston, May 16

● *A.B. (New York)*

The Editors of Freedom,

'A Pacifist Viewpoint on Assassination' (Freedom, May 7th) is an apology for justifiable murder. As such, it knocks the props out of the Anarchist fight against capital punishment. For if Verwoerd can be justifiably murdered, why not the justifiable murder by the State of a murderer?

G. makes a great point of the assassin acting on his own responsibility. Agreed. But the importance of this statement escapes G. completely. The individual can not only choose to murder, but he can also choose *not to murder*. It is imperative that people come to realize that such a choice is open to them in the atomic age.

A man – one man – an assassin, if you will – will release the bomb that shall begin the destruction of our world. Let that man

choose not to murder. Let all of us as individuals help him in that
choice, so that that man – one man – one assassin, may help us.

G.'s choice of justifiable murder brings the day of total murder
that much closer to every one of us.

Sincerely,

A.B.

New York City, May 27, 1960

● *Ernie Crosswell*

Dear Editors,

You suggested in your 'Reply from the Editors' (FREEDOM, May
22) that counter-violence may be an effective policy for coloured
South Africans. I suggest that this is not sound reasoning in view
of the fact that such policies have resulted in the last big violent
line-up - West versus East, with destruction threatened to all of the
human race. Surely another way - if there is one - must be tried.
You expose *Peace News* and T.S. so beautifully and then commit
hara-kiri! Is this the view of all of the Editors?

Ernie Crosswell

Slough, May 22, 1960

● *Albert Meltzer*

Dear Editor,

It might be always more to the point when discussing the so-
called Pacifists, just as with the so-called Communists, to deal
with their record rather than with their alleged principles. The
Pacifist movement in this country has nothing to do with non-
violent resistance and everything to do with opportunist politics
and permeation of the left-wing movement with 'Father Gapons'.

There are some sincere members of the PPU no doubt, such as
those who try to reconcile their consciences by selling *Peace News*
and FREEDOM - how wrong it is of you to 'embarrass' these poor

souls by taking an anarchist point of view in FREEDOM! But the *Observer* would not embarrass them, as it combines militant liberalism with patriotism.

Note how the case of Mr. David Pratt shows them in their true colours. L. Otter and Arlo Tatum, it seems, know all about him - strange they never mentioned him before this incident and that their knowledge of his peculiar ways tallies with the statements issued by the press relations branch of the South African police! Can it be that they have no intention of boycotting this most typical South African product? But even if these slanders were true - is that why they attack Mr Pratt? One can usually evoke some sympathy from the Pacifists for the most diabolical criminal - Neville Heath, John Christie, Rudolf Hess - but striking at the rotten head of a foul dictatorship, one who might by now have been military dictator, is a crime which puts a man beyond the pale in their eyes.

T.S. alarms me when he says that 'logically' if you defend David Pratt you must favour an attentat on Macmillan. He cannot possible mean to suggest that there is any comparison between Macmillan on the one hand and Verwoerd on the other, whether Macmillan believed in apartheid or not. If he did think it in the least feasible, it would hardly be practical to make that remark publicly. But he does not think so. This is the classic remark of the 'Father Gapon' - some of the Holy Willies the PPU have brought into the 'left' could tell him, perhaps, that it was scarcely original to point out so blatantly that *if you do not crucify this man Pratt, you are no friend of Caesar's.*
Albert Meltzer

London, May 17, 1960

Donald Rooum

Assassination

In your reply to Arlo Tatum's letter (FREEDOM 14th May 1960) you decline to discuss his last paragraph about 'a doddering old anarchist who has failed to keep up with the times', etc. on the grounds that it is too childish to be taken seriously. I think this is a pity, as it would be interesting to know whether he means that your attitude of opposition to assassination as a principle combined with sympathy for the assassin is reminiscent of the old FREEDOM, or whether he supposes that anarchists some time ago were the advocates of assassination as a policy.

If the former, Mr. Tatum is quite right. There is still in print* a reprint of a FREEDOM article in 1893 in which assassination was discussed and it was made quite clear that the then editors were utterly opposed to assassination:

The man who in ordinary circumstances and in cold blood would commit such deeds is simply a homicidal maniac; nor do we believe they can be justified upon any mere ground of expediency. Least of all do we think that any human being has a right to egg on another person to such a course of action. We accept the phenomena of homicidal outrage as among the most terrible facts of human experience; we endeavour to look such facts full in the face with the understanding of humane justice; and we believe that we are doing our utmost to put an end to them by spreading Anarchist ideas throughout society.

They were, however, sympathetic to the odd anarchists and others who made individual attempts on the lives of individual tyrants, in much the same way as we sympathise with David Pratt:

Anarchism and Homicidal Outrage,
in 'What is Anarchism?' (Freedom Press, £1.95)

We hate murder with a hatred that may seem absurdly exaggerated to apologists for Matabele massacres, to callous acquiescers in hangings and bombardments, but we decline, in such cases of homicide or attempted homicide as those of which we are treating, to be guilty of the cruel injustice of flinging the whole responsibility of the deed upon the immediate perpetrator. The guilt of these homicides lies upon every man and woman who, intentionally or by cold indifference, helps to keep up social conditions that drive human beings to despair. The man who flings his whole soul into the attempt, at the cost of his own life, to protest against the wrongs of his fellow men, is a saint compared to the active and passive upholders of cruelty and injustice, even if his protest destroy other lives besides his own. Let him who is without sin in society cast the first stone at such an one.

But it is quite possible that Mr. Tatum believes, in common with many others, that the anarchists were once a large bomb-throwing group, committed to assassination as a matter of principle, who declined into a small 'philosophical' sect about 1914. This is the current form of the bomb-thrower myth, a development of the ridiculous fantasy about murderous secret armies of anarchists which was invented at the turn of the century. Who invented this myth, why they invented it and how it achieved popular acceptance has been the subject of a lecture to the LAG and may, if you are interested, be the subject of an article from FREEDOM. Meanwhile it should be reiterated that the myth has no basis in fact.

London, May 16, 1960

Editorial

David Pratt Defends his Act

T he trial of David Pratt started last week in Pretoria but was
adjourned for a fortnight by order of the judge so that the
accused could be committed for observation at a mental institute.
It might seem a little surprising that having kept Mr. Pratt in prison
for the past five months the court should wait until now before
ordering a mental report. However, the reports that have appeared
of the two days hearing before the Supreme Court indicate that
whatever Pratt's family and their advisers may be trying to do to
save him from the legal consequences of his actions, he steadfastly
refuses to either apologise or recant. One of the witnesses, Professor Hirst, declared that 'Pratt recognised that he was doing wrong
when he shot Verwoerd. But in the terms of his belief he felt it was
for the country's good, so he could set this consideration aside.'
Pratt himself told the Court that he did not shoot at Verwoerd 'as
a person'. 'I shot at apartheid' he said, 'the stinking monster of
apartheid which was gripping South Africa by the throat'.

In a further statement he said:

When police and doctors had finished with me and I was pushed into a
cell, I had my best night's sleep for six years. From then until now I have
spent my life in the isolation of a cell with short exercise breaks. Five
months seldom seeing the sun - conditions I never before experienced.
Yet these five months have been a hundred times happier than the past
five years.

If you live in guilt you are never free. If you know you must do
something and you don't do it you are not free.

Of his 'abnormalities' (which we reported at length in last
week's FREEDOM) he spoke 'eloquently' but added 'To me my
abnormalities do not represent insanity'.

And he then told the Court what his message for South African
was and had been since 1954.

Every South African - Afrikaner, English-speaking, coloured, Indian, African and Malay - must play his part if we are to build South Africa, as I know can be done.

South Africa must throw off the slimy snake of apartheid. Practical apartheid cannot go immediately, but the principle must go now.

Pratt then turned to the judge saying: 'Thank you, my lord. That is all I have to say'.

It is ironical that David Pratt is now in a mental institute having his mind probed while the advocates of racial segregation, of apartheid, are occupying the armchairs of government in South Africa obliging others to carry out their inhuman and disgusting policies.

September 24, 1960

Editorial

The David Pratt Trial

B y the time this issue of FREEDOM is published, the trial of David Pratt the wealthy farmer who attempted the life of the South African Premier, Dr. Verwoerd, may have taken place and his fate sealed. According to reports from Johannesburg efforts are being made by his family to persuade the Pretoria Supreme Court that he is suffering from mental disorder and that he should be sent for observation. In support of the plea was David Pratt's account of the shooting which he gave to Professor L.A. Hurst, Professor of Psychological Medicine of Witwatersrand University. The following is the report of it published in last Sunday's *Observer*.

The day before the shooting - according to the professor's account of what Pratt told him - the farmer saw a van into which about 100 prisoners were being put. He thought: 'What the hell will be happening next? This cannot go on. Where can we see any light?'

Pratt then first experienced what he described as 'a feeling'. The next morning 'the feeling became very strong that someone in this country must do something about it, and it better bloody well be me, feeling as I do about it.'

He did not, however, know what to do. Pratt was going to the Rand Show to see about his trout exhibits and before leaving his farm he slipped a 0.22 revolver into his pocket. But he had no definite intention of using it.

At the show he went to the members' stand, spoke briefly to some cattle breeders and then went for a 'spot of lunch'. Pratt then returned to the stand and listened to the Prime Minister's speech. He was 'not impressed'.

The 'feeling' got stronger. He thought: 'What is the country going to do?'There was no applause, no enthusiasm. Nobody was prepared either to cheer or to boo. They were completely negative. 'If there had been strong booing it would have been sufficient.'

He walked to the cattle ring to see three friends, but could not rouse any enthusiasm for conversation. The thought occurred to him: 'What is all this leading to?' Next he thought: 'I shall not kill the man, but lay him up for a month or more to give him time to think things over'.

Then thinking that when a plunge had to be taken it should be taken quickly, Pratt walked up to the stand, pulled out the gun, pointed it and fired it when close to the Prime Minister. (Pratt indicated a distance of 1 ft.)

The farmer is uncertain as to the interval that elapsed before the firing of the second shot. He remembers his hand being bumped and heard the gun going off a second time. 'It all became rather confused after the second shot.'

Pratt added: 'I was grabbed by a number of policemen, pushed around, handcuffed and brought here'. By 'here' he was referring to the South African medico-legal laboratories where he was examined by Professor Hurst.

In addition he told Professor Hurst of the fits from which he had suffered since the age of eight:

These were of a severe type, in which he lost consciousness, fell to the ground and sometimes bit his tongue, and also a milder type.

During the less severe attacks he had twisted an ankle or broken the stem of a wine glass that he happened to be holding. Attacks occurred about once a month, but from 1954 to 1959 they became less frequent. This phase coincided with a general mental change, which Pratt described as euphoria, 'in which the grass looked greener and the birds sang more sweetly'.

After this came a phase of depression which responded to one electro-shock treatment. Pratt identified yet another phase when he was given different treatment. He described himself as 'cured', but changed it to 'much improved', because of a major seizure two or three weeks before the Verwoerd shooting.

Pratt was on horseback at his farm. He was quarrelling with his manager when, without warning, he must have had a minor fit because he found himself on the ground.

The farmer explained that one reason why he was silent and uncommunicative at the Rand Show (10 days after the declaration of a state of emergency) was because of a conviction that 'someone must sacrifice himself'.

When his euphoria came on in 1954 he felt like the prophets in the Bible. He wanted to give away all he possessed and speak intensely against nationalism.

Instead he decided to form a coalition Government. He intended to approach three political leaders, but approached only two, one of whom agreed in principle but the other turned him down. He regretted afterwards he had not consulted the third man, Mr. N.C. Havenga, late leader of the Afrikaner party.

Professor Hurst's report said: 'His current lack of judgement and insight into his limitations at that time, as well as his currently assumed role of political saviour and martyr, lead me to the conclusion that he is at present suffering from a grandiose delusion trend of megalomania'.

In 1954, Pratt said, he heard 'organ music playing in my head'. The experience developed and he began to feel disembodied as if he were looking down on his body. He entered a hospital for nervous disorders, but became violent and smashed windows and had to be locked up.

Then he descended into what he describes as 'a Miltonian hell, complete with fires, prongs and yells of anguish'. He entered a state in which the whole world was a 'play', and everyone was acting.

Whatever impression the account of his fits and state of mind may leave with the reader, that part of his account which deals with the motives behind his decision to shoot Dr. Verwoerd, seem to us perfectly sane and praiseworthy.

September 24, 1960

Editorial

David Pratt Insane?

The Supreme Court in committing David Pratt to Pretoria jail
without trial, on the grounds that the judge found him to be
'mentally disordered and an epileptic', took the easy line out of
what might well have been an embarrassing situation for Mr.
Verwoerd and his segregationist friends. The medical report on
Mr. Pratt's behaviour during the fortnight he was under observation makes unconvincing reading. According to the BUP account:

It said that Pratt was 'completely out of touch with reality', mentally
disordered and an epileptic. Pratt was said to have threatened nurses at the
institution and on one occasion he did not want to drink his tea because he
believed it was poisoned.

Professor Lamont said that he noticed a tattoo mark on Pratt's right
forearm consisting of crossed swords and a date above and below - 9.4.60
and 12.9.60 - with the letter V on one side. Pratt had told him that the V
stood for Verwoerd and the dates indicated his own period of isolation.
Professor Lamont said Pratt's mood was 'one of euphoria combined with
ecstasy'.

Professor Lamont said that Pratt's tendency to minimise his trouble
was an indication that he was completely out of touch with reality. Had
it not been for his wealth, Pratt would most probably have been in
trouble before.

Most people outside South Africa are of the opinion that Mr.
Verwoerd's policy of apartheid is 'completely out of touch with
reality' yet no one has suggested that Mr. Verwoerd is 'mentally
disordered'. The tattoo marks do not seem so strange to us; why
should not those five months have been as meaningful to David
Pratt as the love affair of somebody's sailor boy who then pro-
ceeds to have the event tattooed on his arm? Every prison cell wall
in the world has recorded on it the dates of occupation by its
unhappy inmates.

As to Pratt's 'tendency to minimise the trouble' being an indication that he was 'out of touch with reality' we cannot help thinking of humble as well as famous people who have faced grave situations, in which even their lives may have been at stake, calmly and serenely, and who were at the same time more sane than most of us. After all, one has only to think of Socrates' last thirty days of life to question the prison psychologists's conclusions about those who find peace of mind in spite of their 'crimes'!

David Pratt is now safely put away; the charges against him remain on the files. Is that the end of the story? Will no voice be raised on his behalf against permitting him to rot in jail, his generous action dismissed as that of a 'mentally disordered man'?

For those who have short memories let us repeat David Pratt's statement to the Supreme Court when he appeared before it a fortnight ago:

These five months have been a hundred times happier than the past five years. If you live in guilt you are never free. If you know you must do something and you don't do it you are not free.

The writer of this column salutes David Pratt and despises his detractors!

October 1 1960

Editorial

David Pratt

David Pratt, the Surrey-born farmer who eighteen months ago made an attempt on the life of Dr. Verwoerd, Prime Minister of South Africa and chief architect of the government's hateful policy of apartheid was found dead in his cell in a Bloemfontein mental institution. He is alleged to have committed suicide and to have left a note which read:

Under the circumstances it is the best solution for my problem for everyone. If possible please arrange for a quiet cremation. Please avoid all publicity so that my children can simply be told their father died in hospital.

Though charged with attempted murder, the trial did not take place, the judge declaring that he was an epileptic and mentally disordered, and after spending six months in jail he was transferred to a mental hospital. Last January he asked to be tried but his request was refused. He said that it was 'soul destroying' to be in a mental hospital because he had nothing to do and felt the need for companionship.

The David Pratt case is now closed. Ignored or condemned by those who should have defended his generous act while he was still alive, somehow we feel that the time will come when he will be remembered along with all those who have taken a stand against what David Pratt so truly called 'the stinking monster of apartheid which is gripping the throat of South Africa'.

October 7, 1961

Appendix 1

Martyn Everett

A short history of political violence in Britain

This account of the history of political violence in Britain is written in the political context of the campaign against the poll-tax, and against the background of the massive bombing of Iraq, which has been a feature of the Gulf War. While endorsing the use of mass violence on the international scene, leaders of both Labour and Conservative parties have condemned what they describe as 'political violence' by opponents of the poll-tax, following several robust demonstrations which have been attacked by the police. Such condemnations of 'political violence' have assumed a ritualistic nature, as the politicians seek to deflect criticism away from the original issues, and away from the perpetrators of the real violence in our society.

There is no excuse ever for people to turn to violence ... People who 'turn to violence are against the people and against democracy' stated Margaret Thatcher on April Fools Day.[1]

Strangely, these denunciations are never directed at the arms traders, who pour money into Conservative Party coffers,[2] or against the torturers and dictators who are equipped and armed by the British state and British industry. Those who research and manufacture chemical weapons, or maintain Britain's nuclear arsenal, not only escape criticism, but are defended by both Tory and L:abour politicians alike.

My purpose in writing this short history is to demonstrate that *political violence is a tradition in Britain*. It is a tradition of the British state, the British ruling class, and the institutional pillars of British society. There is a sense in which the whole structure of political and economic life in Britain is underwritten by violence, and to such an extent that the existing social order could not be maintained without it. I have outlined this institutionalised

1. BBC TV News. 9.55pm 1st April, 1990
2. Everett, Martyn: *Big Business Terrorism*, Saffron Walden, 1987 (reprinted from *Black Flag*).

violence elsewhere,[3] so my intention in this tract is to focus on the
direct use of physical violence as a weapon of the state. In order to
highlight grounds of military expediency. With minor exceptions
I have also excluded the use of political violence by the state in
Ireland and Scotland, as it is the violence of a colonial power, and
as such deserves a special study, as does the response to that
colonial violence.

The British ruling class has never been slow to resort to violence to protect its interests, privilege and power. It has done so
throughout history, and it has been real, bloody, violence, not just
violence against property, but violence directed against ordinary
men, women and children, who have sought freedom, equality and
an end to social injustice and poverty.

In fact, the modern British state was founded on violence, and
owes its existence to one of the bloodiest invasions in European
history – the Norman Conquest. After the initial invasion and early
victories, William of Normandy had found it almost impossible to
subdue the north of England, so undertook the sustained and
systematic genocide of the population. According to the chroni-
cler Orderic Vitalis, who journeyed with the Norman invaders:

During this awful time, it is said that 100,000 people perished. It was
terrible to see rotting corpses covered in multitudes of worms in the silent
dwellings and deserted streets and roads made foul by the stench of
putrification. Nobody remained to bury the corpses. On the once bustling
road from York to Durham, there was not a single inhabited village as far
as the eye could see. Nothing moved in the scorched ruins of the villages
but the packs of wolves and wild dogs which tore apart the human corpses.

In Yorkshire alone, out of 1,900 places mentioned in the
Domesday Book, 850 were entirely destroyed, and 300 others
partly wasted. The Normans systematically murdered and destroyed every peasant village and farm until only isolated pockets
of life survived in remote corners.[4]

Historians gloss over this deliberate savagery. The *Encyclopae-
dia Britannica* notes:

Apart from the tragedy of the dispossessed old English aristocracy,

3. Everett, Martyn: *The Military Industrial Complex*, BA Thesis, Cambridge
    College of Arts & Technology, 1981. (Extracts from the above have been
    published in *Peace News*, and in the *Socialist Society Journal* (Cambridge).
4. Bishop, T A M, cited in Muir, Richard: *Lost Villages of Britain*, 1982.

probably the most regrettable effect of the Conquest was the total eclipse of the English vernacular as the language of literature, law and administration.

The thousands of slaughtered people are not mentioned, and their deaths obviously not regretted as much as the dispossession of the English aristocracy!

The Norman conquest was not limited to the destruction of the old English aristocracy, it ushered in a whole new socio-economic order, based on the enforced serfdom of a cowed and decimated population. The Anglo-Saxons were forced into feudal slavery, and all attempts at resistance were ruthlessly suppressed. Feudalism was virtually unknown in pre-conquest England. The so-called Norman 'achievement'[5] was built on the rotting corpses of the English peasantry.

The recently celebrated *Domesday Book* is a record of the enslavement of a whole population, and it is a measure of the 'success' of the Norman invaders in establishing a new ruling-class, that the latter could, 900 years later, hoodwink the British people into celebrating an instrument of their slavery. The Norman aristocracy, the new ruling class, was installed in power so firmly that in spite of civil wars, and armed conflicts between various factions within the ruling class, usurpation, and the almost endemic murder of rivals, it has been able to adapt, absorb and survive right down to the present time.

Using their monopoly of armed force, the Normans instituted severe laws intended to destroy the economic independence of ordinary people, and enforce their participation in new methods of exploitation. The notorious forest laws introduced by the Normans deprived people of access to a major resource. Edicts, like those forbidding ordinary peasants from owning or using handmills, backed by the forcible seizure and smashing of millstones in peasant possession ensured that the common people were forced to use the watermills of the Lord of the Manor, or the local Abbey, paying extortionate dues for the 'pleasure'. Similar actions were taken to prevent drapers setting up their own fulling stocks to press material, forcing them to use the Lord's fulling-mill.[6]

5. This phrase is used by numerous historians, see for example, *Illustrated Dictionary of British History*, ed. by Arthur Marwick, London, 1980 and Cassady, Richard F: *The Norman Achievement*, 1986.
6. Bloch, Marc: 'The advent and triumph of the watermill' in Bloch, Marc: *Land and Work in Medieval Europe*, 1967.

The next time you hear a Tory politician bemoaning the dependency culture spawned by the welfare state, remember that the powerful enforce dependency because it is in their interest. They ensure our dependency by monopolising the means of production, through the threat or use of force. To gain access to the resources we need we are forced to enter into relationships which ensure our continued dependency and subordination.[7]

Violence has not only been used as a tool of oppression across the class boundaries, but also as a way of resolving conflict within the ruling class, as different factions have struggled to assert their supremacy. Feudalism lent itself to factional strife, and during the period when the state depended upon the Church for its administrative structure, the rivalries and intrigues were compounded. The murder of Thomas Becket, on the instructions of Henry II, was echoed down the ages precisely because it exemplifies the conflict between church and state over the balance of power.

We can see that from the formation of the English state, violence has been used to create the basic form of the economy, and to ensure people's forced involvement in that economy. It has also been used to determine who runs the economy, and benefits from that control. At crucial moments in history, the state and the ruling class have resorted to savage slaughter in order to maintain the system when it has been threatened by rebellion from below. During such moments, previously antagonistic sections of the ruling class unite against the common threat to their power and wealth. One such instance was the reaction of the powerful to the Peasants Revolt of 1381.

The Peasants Revolt took place after the Black Death had decimated the labouring population. The government attempted to regulate wages, which had risen dramatically as landlords competed with each other for the available free labour. Court extravagances remained undiluted, and the young Richard II soon found himself embroiled in a war with the French (the Hundred Years War). To finance both extravagances and war, Richard levied a poll-tax. The combined effect of wage-restrictions and poll-tax provoked widespread revolt and the peasants marched on London. The Revolt, and the trickery used to murder Wat Tyler (one of the

7. For an understanding of how dependency works now, see *In and Against the State*, Rev. ed., 1980.

peasant spokesmen), has been widely documented,[8] but the savage reprisals that followed the failure of the Peasants Revolt are frequently neglected. The Victorian historian, J.R. Green estimated that 7,000 people were killed in the wake of the revolt.[9] Those peasants caught were slaughtered on the spot, or dragged to the centre of the nearest town or village and beheaded. Many were hung, drawn and quartered; and because there was a shortage of gibbets, frequently hung, nine or ten to a single beam. The old feudal order was restored and maintained by the blood of its victims.

The Peasants Revolt was not an aberration. England's history has been punctuated by an almost continuous series of rebellions, insurrections, revolts and riots. That historians have presented them as isolated incidents has helped to deny their legitimacy, reduced our recognition of their positive impact, and drawn attention away from the continual and consistent threat of state violence that has been the response of the ruling class and the state. The Pilgrimage of Grace, the Kent and Cornish risings, and Kett's Norfolk rebellion were all marked by the savagery of the repression which followed their failure.[10]

Violence has been crucial in ensuring that the rich hang on to their power and wealth, keeping the poor 'in their place'. A.L. Beier notes that during the Tudor period, poverty, homelessness and a refusal of subservience were all punishable offences. Vagrancy had been created by the Tudor policies of enclosure and the break-up of the monasteries. Vagrants, who formed part of a rootless, embryonic pre-working class were seen as a threat because they were not coerced by the normal sanctions of feudalism. It was a crime to be a 'masterless man', and vagrants could (at various times) be whipped, or have a one-inch hole 'bored through the gristle of the right ear with a hot iron'.[11] Other forms of corporal punishment included hair-pulling, the pillory, the ducking stool, ear-cropping, and hanging.

As religion and the Church occupied an important position within the power structure, it was vital to the power elite to

8. A most readable short account can be found in Poulson, Charles: *The English Rebels*, 1984.
9. Green, J R.:*Short History of the English People*, 1893.
10. Poulson: op. cit.
11. Beier, A L: *Masterless Men*, 1985.

maintain religious loyalty and conformity; hence, for example, the persecution of the Lollards as heretics. With the Reformation the situation became more complex: loyalty to the Church could collide with loyalty to the King, as Thomas More discovered. Religion increasingly became the battleground for rival factions of the ruling class, so persecution of Protestants alternated with persecution of Catholics. During the short reign of Mary I (1553-58) there were nearly 300 Protestants burnt at the stake, while in the years that followed countless Catholics were persecuted, imprisoned and killed because of their faith.

The persecution of people according to their religion was soon outdone by the persecutions for witchcraft, which proved to be the ideal instrument for controlling the growing numbers of dissident, almost atheistic disbelievers. Witchcraft became a criminal offence in the 16th century, and by the time of the repeal of the Witchcraft statutes in 1736, over 1,000 people in England, and 4,000 people in Scotland had been executed for witchcraft.[12]

By the middle of the 17th century the gradual development of capitalism had resulted in the emergence of new classes, with different interests from those of the feudal aristocracy, and eventually the antagonisms between them spilt over into civil war and revolution. The conduct of the Civil War forms no part of this short survey, but the Revolution which paralleled the Civil War, and frequently threatened to transform it, does deserve scrutiny. In the social space created the fracturing of the ruling class monopoly on power, new ideas emerged, and old ideas were given new forms: the 'Good Old Cause' of Liberty and Democracy was expanded to create a form of socialism which is the forerunner of our own. The Levellers and the Diggers (also known as the True Levellers) outlined a social programme which would have created a world vastly different, and more humane, than the world we inhabit. They weren't defeated because the objective conditions were wrong, or because they were ahead of their time. On the contrary, their proposals were a practical solution to the problems of their time. They were defeated by the use of physical force.

Even prior to the Civil War, many of the most radical and dissident elements required immense courage to persist in their beliefs in the face of the vicious violence meted out by Charles I

---

12. MacFarlane, Alan: *Witchcraft in Tudor and Stuart England*, 1970. Thomas, K.: *Religion and the Decline of Magic*, 1978.

and his courts. William Prynne had his ears cut off, for sedition, and then had the remaining stumps cropped because of his persistence. In fact, he continued preaching a sermon outlining his beliefs, while undergoing the punishment. John Lilburne was frequently imprisoned and flogged. Once he was flogged all the way from the Fleet Bridge (now Ludgate Circus) to Westminster, before being placed in the pillory. He remained defiant, and was chained in prison. So refractory was Lilburne that he was imprisoned several times under Cromwell as well.

The Levellers and the Diggers fought on the Parliamentary side, and their ideas became increasingly popular, to the dismay of Cromwell and other Grandees, as at times it looked as if this movement would actually take over. Cromwell, although prepared to challenge the political structure of the country, did not wish to see a radical change in either economy or society, so met the challenge in several ways – by appeals to loyalty and unity in the face of the Royalist enemy; by ensuring that the most troublesome regiments and individuals were drafted to fight in Ireland; and by violent suppression. After the Putney debates, Col. Rainsborough proposed a parade of the whole army at Ware, in order to settle Leveller demands for democracy and equality. At this parade one regiment of foot soldiers marched in, the Leveller 'Agreement of the People' stuck in their hats. They marched past without orders, shouting for its implementation and demanding 'Justice! Soldiers Rights! Freedom!'. Cromwell, with sword drawn had fourteen arrested, and after a drumhead court martial, one soldier, Richard Arnold, was shot on the spot. Cromwell had already had Leveller leaders like Lilburne imprisoned in an attempt to destroy Leveller influence in the army. At Bishopsgate radical soldiers protesting arrears of pay, were arrested and 23 year old Robert Lockyer was shot in St. Paul's Churchyard. His body was followed to the grave by thousands of Londoners, all wearing the sea-green ribbon of the Levellers.[13]

Leveller mutinies at Banbury, Burford and Salisbury demanded acceptance of the 'Agreement', but Cromwell managed to prevent the disparate groups linking up and attacked them at night. Captain Thompson their flamboyant leader refused to surrender, and was hunted down, before being shot in the back.[14] At Burford three

13. Brailsford, H N: *The Levellers and the English Revolution*, 1961.
14. Poulson: op. cit.

corporals were imprisoned in the church, and shot the next day.

The strategy of the Diggers was deliberately non-violent: cultivating the common land and sharing the benefits amongst all, yet they were attacked time and time again. Their shelters were destroyed, and their crops spoilt. Sometimes they were arrested, and eventually they were forced to abandon their attempts to establish a free communist society. It is quite apparent that the people who rule society can never allow people to demonstrate the success of running their own lives. That is a 'threat' they cannot tolerate.

The use of force by the power elite[15] is a constant feature of politics in Britain. Changes in government, or variations of the ideological justification for the use of state violence make little or no difference. Consequently the Restoration did not terminate the use of violence as a means of exerting state power. When the Duke of Monmouth attempted to seize the throne from James II he provided a rallying point for all the disaffected people who had been appalled by the return of the monarchy: Levellers, Fifth Monarchists and other dissidents flocked to Monmouth's standard. The repression which followed the failure of Monmouth's attempt at the crown was savage: of the 6,000 who marched out of Taunton with Monmouth, more than 1,000 were killed, died of wounds or were hanged in the immediate aftermath of Sedgmoor. This butchery was followed by the infamous Bloody Assizes, conducted by the equally infamous Judge Jeffreys.

Nearly 2,000 people were dealt with during the Bloody Assizes, of whom Jeffreys sentenced to death about 300 (250 of whom were executed) and some 800 more to transportation. Jeffreys brutal conduct during the trial, and the blatant profiteering from the transportations by royal courtiers provided an added twist of the knife. Even young school-girls were taken as hostages by the state, and would have been transported except that their parents paid a huge bribe to the Queen's ladies-in-waiting, to whom they had been 'given'. Some of the condemned prisoners were saved from death simply because the sheer numbers to be executed were too high for the executioners to cope. According to Robert Milne-Tyte, out of one group of 29 men who were

---

15. I use the term power elite in the sociological sense pioneered by C. Wright Mills, to identify an alliance of interests within the ruling class, through which the ruling class exercises its power.

sentenced to death only 13 were executed 'probably because the sheer physical task of hanging and quartering as many as 29 was simply beyond Jack Ketch and his assistant Pascha Rose, whose normal job was the bloodily appropriate one of butcher'. In an attempt to intimidate the population, the butchered quarters of the victims were publicly exhibited across the country (in 35 towns and villages in Somerset alone).[16]

Not only was the framework of the British state forged with violence, and maintained by violence, when social and economic changes have necessitated an accommodation between different classes and class-factions, the state has been violently restructured. The Wars of the Roses resulted in the development of Tudor absolutism, which by creating the conditions for the accelerated growth of an incipient capitalism led in turn to the emergence of new classes, whose interests conflicted with those of the absolutist monarchy. The Civil War, the Restoration, and Monmouth's rebellion were the bloody signposts pointing towards the restructured balance of class forces that was achieved by the 'Glorious Revolution'. Predictably, this recomposition of the power elite excluded the working classes.

Massive violence, on a scale inconceivable to anyone except the direct victims was also used to create the economic system we know as capitalism. Of course, classical economy was based on military rule, and force was the keystone of the feudal economies of Europe. Within those societies characterised as hydraulic, the monopoly of violence enjoyed by the ruling groups was also crucial.[17] So capitalism is not unusual in its use of force, but it is remarkable in the extent to which force has been used to restructure the economy on a global scale.

The development of colonialism was central to the rapid industrialisation of Europe in terms of cheap and often new raw materials, as well as providing growing markets for manufactured goods. Colonialism also provided the infrastructure necessary for the growing development of capitalism as a global economy, dependent on Europe (and later Europe and North America). Britain played a major part in the colonial expansion of Europe. Indigenous populations were frequently slaughtered on a massive scale, and established local economies were destroyed. Millions of

16. Milne-Tyte, Robert: *Bloody Jeffrey's – the Hanging Judge*, 1989.
17. Wittfogel, Karl: *Oriental Despotism*, 1957.

people, in what we now call the Third World were sold, or forced into slavery. The people who survived became one commodity among the many commodities that enriched the economies of Europe, and Britain in particular.[18] It should be said that it was the rich and powerful who were lining their pockets, because the plight of working people in Britain was often desperate, so the whole of the 18th century, and the early parts of the 19th century were rocked by wave after wave of hunger riots.

The sheer size of the British Empire was not accidental, but the result of harnessing military power to international trade. The restructuring of the conquered economies, the access to cheap raw materials, and slave labour would not have been possible without the systematic deployment of violence – on a massive scale. The colonisation of Africa, Asia, North and South America and Australasia was not a piecemeal affair, but a highly disciplined process, organised and supported by the British state through the use of military power. The much vaunted individual initiative came in primarily when it was time to line a few private pockets.

During the whole of this period domestic political dominance was maintained by the use of force, corruption, and the structured use of poverty to ensure the exclusion of the working class from political life. Violence was typically deployed by only one side in the class struggle – the ruling class. There was, for example, the St. George's Fields massacre of the 10th May, 1768, when troops opened fire on demonstrators for 'Wilkes and Liberty', outside the gaol in which Wilkes was imprisoned. Soldiers fired into the crowd, killing several and wounding others. Twelve years later, during what have been called the 'Gordon Riots', the population of London attacked the prisons, freeing the prisoners and burning the prisons down. The widespread rioting also resulted in the destruction of the homes of particularly repressive agents of the state, such as notorious judges. Accounts of the riots are detailed, yet do not record a single death caused by the demonstrators – yet the state responded with harsh, systematic repression, killing an estimated 850 people, and imprisoning or transporting many more.[19]

During the 18th and 19th centuries the power elite retained its power by exercising its monopoly of political violence. Demonstrations were pronounced to be riots, criminalising the demonstrators,

18. Genovese, Eugene D.: *The World the Slaveholders Made*, 1970.
19. Nicholson, John: *The Great Liberty Riot of 1780*, 1985.

and legitimising the beatings and killings which were directed against them. The incidents were numerous. Among the most serious were the following:

1766 Bread riots. Troops kill 13. 200 arrested.

1768 St. George's Fields massacre. Soldiers shot and killed six, injuring 15.

1780 Gordon Riots. Authorities kill 850. Hundreds imprisoned and transported.

1810 Burdett Riots. One person killed by Life Guards in Piccadilly.

1819 Peterloo, Manchester. Cavalry charge peaceful demonstration. 11 killed, and at least 560 injured.

1821 Queen Caroline Riots. Two shot dead, many injured.

1830s Swing disturbances. Over 2,000 tried, 252 sentenced to death, 19 hung. 505 transported, 644 imprisoned. Battle for free newspapers, nearly 800 imprisoned. Chartism. In ten years 1,400 arrested.

1831 Pro-Reform disturbances. April, Derby, demonstrators attack city gaols releasing prisoners. Military and yeomanry kill three. October, Bristol. Official estimates: 12 killed by troops, 94 wounded, 102 arrests, 34 transported and four executed. Thomas Brereton refuses to fire on demonstrators, and sides with protestors, so is arrested and court martialled. Commits suicide in January, 1832. Unofficial estimates put the numbers killed as high as 500.

1838 North Kent Rising. Police and troops kill 13.

1839 Chartist rising in Newport. Soldiers shoot 20 dead. During 17 months ended May, 1840, 480 persons in England and Wales committed for political crimes. Four-fifths are convicted.

1842 Plug Riots. August, troops fire on crowd in Salford, wounding seven. Young girl killed at Stalybridge, when paving stones thrown at demonstrators outside the mill of Tory yeomanry captain, H. Birley (of Peterloo notoriety). 'The bulk of the lethal violence in the Plug Plot riots came after the government crackdown' (Palmer). Several demonstrators shot and killed, more than 1,100 arrested 749 given prison sentences. Nearly 80 transported (15 for life).

1848   Glasgow food riots. Five shot and killed by military
        pensioners.
1887   Bloody Sunday. Two killed by police in Trafalgar Square.
1893   Featherstone Colliery, Yorkshire. Authorities kill two,
        injure more than ten others.

These state killings took place against a background of general repression, and the criminalisation of what had previously been accepted as legitimate activities. Between 1787 and 1868 162,000 people were transported on convict ships to the Antipodes.[20] According to George Rude between 1810 and 1850 sixty-six people were hung for a variety of protest offences, while E.P. Thompson notes that of those transported, 3,500 were transported for protest crimes.[21]

The repeated use of state violence was reinforced by a deliberate process through which the state criminalised the activities of the working people in order to enforce their dependence: street trading, the performing of plays, dancing etc., even the establishment of coffee houses were all seen as threats which must be controlled, and an elaborate system of licenses was established. Enclosures ensured economic dependence, by depriving people of access to land. Because the enclosure of common land took place over hundreds of years in England, the impact was not as dramatically obvious as the clearances in Scotland, where the short time-scale throws the effects into sharp relief. In a period of only a few years thousands of people were thrown off the land and made homeless. In the case of the Isle of Skye alone, John Prebble[22] records the serving of 1,740 writs of removal affecting 40,000 people between 1840 and 1880. A few years earlier, between 1811 and 1820, an estimated 10,000 people had been evicted from the Sutherland estates on the mainland: many of them literally forced into emigration, taken from their homes to waiting boats. In England, according to Richard Muir: '50,000 or more English villagers tasted the bitterness and hardship of eviction' to make way for the sheep.[23]

20. Slack, Paul, ed: *Rebellion, Popular Protest and the Social Order in Early Modern England*, 1984.
21. Rude, G: *The Crowd in History*, 1981.
     Thompson, E P: *Making of the English Working Class*, 1963.
22. Prebble, J: *Highland Clearances*, 1963.
23. Muir: op. cit.

The twentieth century hasn't really seen a change in heart within the power elite, who remain firmly wedded to the use of state violence as a political weapon. In 1911 troops opened fire on demonstrating strikers in Liverpool and Llanelli, killing four. These shootings during the waves of syndicalist strikes were to be dwarfed by the violence that followed three years later.

The senseless slaughter of hundreds of thousands of people during the fighting between rival imperial systems during World War I provides grimly adequate testimony to the way in which the state (not only in Britain) controls and organises the means of destruction, creating mass institutions for the systematic regulation of violence and death. Those people who opposed this wholesale killing were branded as cowards, physically attacked and beaten up by mobs which were covertly encouraged and organised by the British government.[24] Conscientious objectors were conscripted and imprisoned, or bullied into becoming stretcher-bearers, which frequently resulted in their deaths. In several cases people who refused to fight (often Quakers) were physically transported to the front-line, and when they refused to kill, were shot for desertion. Others, who cracked-up under fire, or who came to their senses when they witnessed the horrors of trench warfare and refused to fight, were also shot for desertion. Many of these official murders occurred under the British Army Act, and are covered by the Official Secrets Act – presumably to protect the bemedalled reputations of both state and its militarist supporters. 'The firing squad victims were overwhelmingly working-class, often ill-educated and inarticulate, and owing to the stress of trench warfare frequently in poor health'.[25] At least 350 men were shot in this way.

In case it should be thought that the state has become more enlightened or tolerant of dissent since the Second World War, it is worth recording the way in which the police have been used during the last twenty years, to break up demonstrations, and crush strikes:

1974   Kevin Gately killed when mounted police baton charged an anti-fascist demonstration in Red Lion Square, London.

1977   Police used to break Grunwick strike. Hundreds arrested.

24. Weller, Ken: Don't Be a Soldier!, 1985.
25. Putowski, Julian & Sykes, Julian: Shot at Dawn, 1989.

1979   Police riot at anti-fascist demonstration in Southall, London, killing Blair Peach. Ten year cover-up begins, to shield those responsible.

1981   Anti-police riots in Brixton and Toxteth. One man is shot in the chest, and a disabled man is deliberately run over by a police vehicle. Police drive vehicles into crowds to make them disperse.

1983   Police used to break print workers' picket in Warrington.

1983/84 Hundreds arrested during the Stop the City demonstrations in financial area of city of London. Police beat up many demonstrators and use trumped-up charges to arrest others. Stop the City demonstrations were directed against the financial involvement of Banks in the arms trade and Third World exploitation.
        This period also results in the arrest of thousands of anti-nuclear activists around the country, and the harassment of peace camps at Greenham Common, Upper Heyford, Faslane, and elsewhere.

1984   The Miners' Strike. More than 10,000 arrested, mostly on trumped-up charges, in a massive police operation to break the strike. Police attack picket lines on numerous occasions.
        Riot police also attack student demonstration at Manchester University against Home Secretary, Leon Brittan. Some students subsequently harassed and threatened by police.

1985   Anti-police riots in Birmingham, Bristol, and Tottenham in London. Police attack and violently break up a 'hippy' convoy near Stonehenge.

1985/86 Print workers' dispute, Wapping. Mounted police charge pickets injuring several.

1988   Mounted police charge student demonstrators on Westminster Bridge, London. Several injured.

1990   Anti-poll tax demonstrations attacked by police. Many injured.

1991   Anti-war protestors arrested.

Because we are continually bombarded with news and information, with incidents remaining topical for only a few hours or days, the pattern does not become obvious until the incidents are listed.

Yet it is clear that the police are regularly used to harass and attack strikers and political opponents of the government.

People who are working for social justice, equality and freedom are instinctively and theoretically opposed to violence, yet naturally will defend themselves and their friends when attacked, if only to repel the attackers and minimise the violence they will suffer. The State's tactics are classical: using the police, as Mussolini used his fascisti to attack demonstrators, break strikes, beat up students, and then condemn the violence of the victims. The defensive violence of the victims is then used as a justification for the violence of the state. Yet there is no real comparison between the two. The violence of the victims is defensive, unorganised and individual, it is also usually unarmed. The violence of the state is massive, systematic, aggressive, and frequently involves the use of sophisticated weapons.

The political representatives of the armed state, with their privileged access to mass-circulation newspapers, and nationally broadcast electronic media, are ready to denounce *some* kinds of violence at the drop of a hat. What they cannot, and will not denounce is the systematic violence that underpins the structure of power they benefit from.

Of course, violence isn't the only means by which the powerful hold on to their power – but the media monopolies, restricted ownership and control of capital, the electoral bribes, the daily processes of exploitation, the legal system, and the petty and suffocating bureaucracies (private and state) would not survive for long unless backed by the threat of their gaols, the violence of their police, the armies of spies and informers, the dirty tricks departments of MI5 and MI6, and the killings they are prepared to inflict with their soldiers.

Their violence is political – but when will they renounce it?

Appendix 2

Errico Malatesta

Anarchism and Violence

Anarchists are opposed to violence; everyone knows that. The main plank of anarchism is the removal of violence from human relations. It is life based on the freedom of the individual, without the intervention of the *gendarme*. For this reason we are enemies of capitalism which depends on the protection of the *gendarme* to oblige workers to allow themselves to be exploited – or even to remain idle and go hungry when it is not in the interest of the bosses to exploit them. We are therefore enemies of the State which is the coercive, violent organisation of society.

But if a man of honour declares that he believes it stupid and barbarous to argue with a stick in his hand and that it is unjust and evil to oblige a person to obey the will of another at pistol point, is it, perhaps, reasonable to deduce that that gentleman intends to allow himself to be beaten up and be made to submit to the will of another without having recourse to more extreme means for his defence?

Violence is justifiable only when it is necessary to defend oneself and others from violence. It is where necessity ceases that crime begins ...

The slave is always in a state of legitimate defence and consequently, his violence against the boss, against the oppressor, is always morally justifiable, and must be controlled only by such considerations as that the best and most economical use is being made of human effort and human sufferings.[1]

There are certainly other men, other parties and schools of thought which are as sincerely motivated by the general good as are the best among us. But what distinguishes the anarchists from all the others is in fact their horror of violence, their desire and intention to eliminate physical violence from human relations ... But why, then, it may be asked, have anarchists in the present

1.   *Umanita Nova* August 25, 1921

struggle [against Fascism] advocated and used violence when it is in contradiction with their declared ends? So much so that many critics, some in good faith, and all who are in bad faith, have come to believe that the distinguishing characteristic of anarchism is, in fact, violence. The question may seem embarrassing, but it can be answered in a few words. For two people to live in peace they must both want peace; if one insists on using force to oblige the other to work for him and serve him, then the other, if he wishes to retain his dignity as a man and not be reduced to abject slavery, will be obliged, in spite of his love of peace, to resist force with adequate means.[2]

The struggle against government is, in the last analysis, physical, material.

Governments make the law. They must therefore dispose of the material forces (police and army) to impose the law, for otherwise only those who wanted to would obey it, and it would no longer be the law, but a simple series of suggestions which all would be free to accept or reject. Governments have this power, however, and use it through the law, to strengthen their power, however, as well as to serve the interests of the ruling classes, by oppressing and exploiting the workers.

The only limit to the oppression of government is the power with which the people show themselves capable of opposing it.

Conflict may be open or latent; but it always exists since the government does not pay attention to discontent and popular resistance except when it is faced with the danger of insurrection.

When the people meekly submit to the law, or their protests are feeble and confined to words, the government studies its own interests and ignores the needs of the people; when the protests are lively, insistent, threatening, the government, depending on whether it is more or less understanding, gives way or resorts to repression. But one always comes back to insurrection, for if the government does not give way, the people will end by rebelling; and if the government does give way, then the people gain confidence in themselves and make ever increasing demands, until such time as the incompatibility between freedom and authority becomes clear and the violent struggle is engaged.

2. *Pensiero e Volontà* September 1, 1924

It is therefore necessary to be prepared, morally and materially, so that when this does happen the people will emerge victorious.[3]

This revolution must of necessity be violent, even though violence is in itself an evil. It must be violent because a transitional, revolutionary, violence, is the only way to put an end to the far greater, and permanent, violence which keeps the majority of mankind in servitude.[4]

The bourgeoisie will not allow itself to be expropriated without a struggle, and one will always have to resort to the *coup de force*, to the violation of legal order by illegal means.[5]

We too are deeply unhappy at this need for violent struggle. We who preach love, and who struggle to achieve a state of society in which agreement and love are possible among men, suffer more than anybody by the necessity with which we are confronted of having to defend ourselves with violence against the violence of the ruling classes. However, to renounce a liberating violence, when it is the only way to end the daily sufferings and the savage carnage which afflict mankind, would be to connive at the class antagonisms we deplore and at the evils which arise from them.[6]

We neither seek to impose anything by force nor do we wish to submit to a violent imposition.

We intend to use force against government, because it is by force that we are kept in subjection by government.

We intend to expropriate the owners of property because it is by force that they withhold the raw materials and wealth, which is the fruit of human labour, and use it to oblige others to work in their interest.

We shall resist with force whoever would wish by force, to retain or regain the means to impose his will and exploit the labour of others.

We would resist with force any 'dictatorship' or 'constituent' which attempted to impose itself on the masses in revolt. And we

3. *Programma Anarchico*, Bologna, July 1920
4. *Umanità Nova*, August 12, 1920
5. *Umanità Nova*, September 9, 1921
6. *Umanità Nova*, April 27, 1920

will fight the republic as we fight the monarchy, if by republic is meant a government, however it may have come to power, which makes laws and disposes of military and penal powers to oblige the people to obey.

With the exception of these cases, in which the use of force is justified as a defence against force, we are always against violence, and for self-determination.[7]

I have repeated a thousand times that I believe that not to 'actively' resist evil, adequately and by every possible way is, in theory absurd, because it is in contradiction with the aim of avoiding and destroying evil, and in practice immoral because it is a denial of human solidarity and the duty that stems from it to defend the weak and the oppressed. I think that a regime which is born of violence and which continues to exist by violence cannot be overthrown except by a corresponding and proportionate violence, and that one is therefore either stupid or deceived in relying on legality where the oppressors can change the law to suit their own ends. But I believe that violence is, for us who aim at peace among men, and justice and freedom for all, an unpleasant necessity, which must cease the moment liberation is achieved – that is, at the point where defence and security are no longer threatened – or become a crime against humanity, and the harbinger of new oppression and injustice.[8]

We are on principle opposed to violence and for this reason wish that the social struggle should be conducted as humanely as possible. But this does mean that we would wish it to be less determined, less thoroughgoing; indeed we are of the opinion that in the long run half measures only indefinitely prolong the struggle, neutralising it as well as encouraging more of the kind of violence which one wishes to avoid. Neither does it mean that we limit the right of self defence to resistance against actual or imminent attack. For us the oppressed are always in a state of legitimate defence and are fully justified in rising without waiting to be actually fired on; and we are fully aware of the fact that attack is often the best means of defence ...

7. *Umanità Nova*, May 9, 1920
8. *Pensiero e Volontà*, April 16, 1925

Revenge, persistent hatred, cruelty to the vanquished when they
have been overcome, are understandable reactions and can even
be forgiven, in the heat of the struggle, in those whose dignity has
been cruelly offended, and whose most intimate feelings have
been outraged. But to condone ferocious anti-human feelings and
raise them to the level of a principle, advocating them as a tactic
for a movement, is both evil and counter-revolutionary.

For us revolution must not mean the substitution of one oppressor for another, of our domination for that of others. We want the
material and spiritual elevation of man; the disappearance of every
distinction between vanquished and conquerors; sincere brother-
hood among all mankind – without which history would continue,
as in the past, to be an alternation between oppression and rebellion, at the expense of real progress, and in the long term to the
disadvantage of everybody, the conquerors no less than the vanquished.[9]

It is abundantly clear that violence is needed to resist the
violence of the adversary, and we must advocate and prepare it, if
we do not wish the present situation of slavery in disguise, in
which most of humanity finds itself, to continue and worsen. But
violence contains within itself the danger of transforming the
revolution into a brutal struggle without the light of an ideal and
without possibilities of a beneficial outcome; and for this reason
one must stress the moral aims of the movement, and the need, and
the duty, to contain violence within the limits of strict necessity.

We do not say that violence is good when we use it and harmful
when others use it against us. We say that violence is justifiable,
good and 'moral' as well as a duty when it is used in ones's own
defence and that of others, against the demands of those who
believe in violence; it is evil and 'immoral' if it serves to violate
the freedom of others ...

We are not 'pacifists' because peace is not possible unless it is
desired by both sides.

We consider violence a necessity and a duty for defence, but
only for defence. And we mean not only for defence against direct,
sudden, physical attack, but against all those institutions which use
force to keep the people in a state of servitude.

9   *Fede!* October 28, 1923

We are against fascism and we would wish that it were weakened by opposing to its violence a greater violence. And we are, above all, against government, which is permanent violence.[10]

To my mind if violence is justifiable even beyond the needs of self-defence, then it is justified when it is used against us, and we would have no grounds for protest.[11]

To the alleged incapacity of the people we do not offer a solution by putting ourselves in the place of the former oppressors. Only freedom or the struggle for freedom can be the school for freedom.

But, you will say, to start a revolution and bring it to its conclusion one needs a force which is also armed. And who denies this? But this armed force, or rather the numerous armed revolutionary groups, will be performing a revolutionary task if they serve to free the people and prevent the re-emergence of an authoritarian government. But they will be tools of reaction and destroy their own achievements if they are prepared to be used to impose a particular kind of social organisation or the programme of a particular party ...[12]

Revolution being, by the necessity of things, violent action, tends to develop, rather than remove, the spirit of violence. But the revolution as conceived by anarchists is the least violent of all and seeks to halt all violence as soon as the need to use force to oppose that of the government and the bourgeoisie, ceases.

Anarchists recognise violence only as a means of legitimate defence; and if today they are in favour of violence it is because they maintain that slaves are always in a state of legitimate defence. But the anarchist ideal is for a society in which the factor of violence has been eliminated, and their ideal serves to restrain, correct and destroy the spirit of revenge which revolution, as a physical act, would tend to develop.

In any case, the remedy would never be the organisation and consolidation of violence in the hands of a government or dictator-

10. *Umanità Nova*, October 21, 1922
11. *Il Risveglio*, December 20, 1922
12. *Fede!*, November 25, 1923

ship, which cannot be founded on anything but brute force and recognition of the authority of police – and military – forces.[13]

... An error, the opposite of the one which the terrorists make, threatens the anarchist movement. Partly as a reaction to the abuse of violence during recent years, partly as a result of the survival of Christian ideas, and above all, as a result of the mystical preachings of Tolstoy, which owe their popularity and prestige to the genius and high moral qualities of their author, anarchists are beginning to pay serious attention to the party of passive resistance, whose basic principle is that the individual must allow himself and others to be persecuted and despised rather than harm the aggressor. It is what has been called *passive anarchy*.

Since there are some, upset by my aversion to useless and harmful violence, who have been suggesting that I displayed tolstoyanism tendencies, I take the opportunity to declare that, in my opinion, this doctrine however sublimely altruistic it may appear to be, is, in fact the negation of instinct and social duties. A man may, if he is a very good ... christian, suffer every kind of provocation without defending himself with every weapon at his disposal, and still remain a moral man. But would he not, in practise, even unconsciously, be a supreme egoist were he to allow others to be persecuted without making any effort to defend them? If, for instance, he were to prefer that a class should be reduced to abject misery, that a people should be downtrodden by an invader, that a man's life or liberty should be abused, rather than bruise the flesh of the oppressor?

There can be cases where passive resistance is an effective weapon, and it would then obviously be the best of weapons, since it would be the most economic in human suffering. But more often than not, to profess passive resistance only serves to reassure the oppressors against their fear of rebellion, and thus it betrays the cause of the oppressed.

It is interesting to observe how both the *terrorists* and the *tolstoyans*, just because both are mystics, arrive at practical results which are more or less similar. The former would not hesitate to destroy half mankind so long as the idea triumphed; the latter would be prepared to let all mankind remain under the yoke of great suffering rather than violate a principle.

13. *Umanità Nova*, July 18, 1920

For myself, I would violate every principle in the world in order to save a man: which would in fact be a question of respecting principle, since, in my opinion, all moral and sociological principles are reduced to this one principle: the good of mankind, the good of all mankind.[14]

14. *Anarchia* (Numero Unico), August, 1896

Attentats

I remember that on the occasion of a much publicised anarchist *attentat* a socialist of the first rank just back from fighting in the Greco-Turkish war, shouted from the housetops with the approval of his comrades, that human life is always sacred and must not be threatened, not even in the cause of freedom. It appeared that he excepted the lives of Turks and the cause of Greek independence. Illogicality, or hypocrisy?[1]

Anarchist violence is the only violence that is justifiable, which is not criminal. I am of course speaking of violence which has truly anarchist characteristics, and not of this or that case of blind and unreasoning violence which has been attributed to anarchists, or which perhaps has been committed by real anarchists driven to fury by abominable persecutions, or blinded by oversensitiveness, uncontrolled by reason, at the sight of social injustices, of suffering for the sufferings of others.

Real anarchist violence is that which ceases when the necessity of defence and liberation ends. It is tempered by the awareness that individuals in isolation are hardly, if at all, responsible for the position they occupy through heredity and environment; real anarchist violence is not motivated by hatred but by love; and noble because it aims at the liberation of all and not at the substitution of one's own domination for that of others.

There is a political party in Italy which, aiming at highly civilised ends, set itself the task of extinguishing all confidence in violence among the masses ... and has succeeded in rendering

1. *Pensiero e Volontà*, September 1, 1924

them incapable of any resistance against the rise of fascism. It seemed to me that Turati himself more or less clearly recognised and lamented the fact in his speech in Paris commemorating Jaurès.

The anarchists are without hypocrisy. Force must be resisted by force: today against the oppression of today; tomorrow against those who might replace that of today.[2]

McKinley, head of North American oligarchy, the instrument and defender of the capitalist giants, the betrayer of the Cubans and the Philippinos, the man who authorised the massacre of the strikers of Hazleton, the torturer of the workers in the 'model republic'; McKinley who incarnated the militaristic, expansionist and imperialist policies on which the fat American bourgeoisie have embarked, has fallen foul of an anarchist's revolver.

If we feel at all distressed it is for the fate in store for the generous-hearted man, who opportunely or inopportunely, for good or tactically bad reasons, gave himself in wholesale sacrifice to the cause of equality and liberty ...

[It might be argued by those who have condemned Czolgosz's act] that the workers' cause and that of the revolution have not been advanced; that McKinley is succeeded by his equal, Roosevelt, and everything remains unchanged except that the situation for anarchists has become a little more difficult than before. And they may be right; indeed, from what I know of the American scene, this will most likely be the case.

What it means is that [as] in war there are brilliant as well as false moves, there are cautious combattants as well as others who are easily carried away by enthusiasm and allow themselves to be an easy target for the enemy, and may even compromise the position of their comrades. This means that each one must advise, defend and practise the methods which he thinks most suitable to achieve victory in the shortest time and with the least sacrifice possible; but it does not alter the fundamental and obvious fact that he who struggles, well or badly, against the common enemy and towards the same goals as us, is our friend and has a right to expect our warm sympathy even if we cannot accord him our unconditional approval.

2. *Pensiero e Volontà*, September 1, 1924

Whether the fighting unit is a collectivity or a single individual cannot change the moral aspect of the problem. An armed insurrection carried out inopportunely can produce real or aparent harm to the social war we are fighting, just as an individual attentat which antagonises popular feeling; but if the insurrection was made to conquer freedom, no one will dare deny the socio-political characteristics of the defeated insurrectionists. Why should it be any different when the insurrectionist is a single individual? ...

It is not a question of discussing tactics. If it were, I would say that in general I prefer collective action to individual action, also because collective action demands qualities which are fairly common and makes the allocation of tasks more or less possible, whereas one cannot count on heroism, which is exceptional and by its nature sporadic, calling for individual sacrifice. The problem here is of a higher order; it is a question of the revolutionary spirit, of that almost instinctive feeling of hatred of oppression, without which programmes remain dead letters however libertarian are the proposals they embody; it is a question of that combative spirit, without which even anarchists become domesticated and end up, by one road or another, in the slough of legalitarianism ... [3]

Gaetano Bresci, worker and anarchist, has killed Humbert, king. Two men: one dead prematurely, the other condemned to a life of torment which is a thousand times worse than death! Two families plunged into sadness!

Whose fault is it? ...

It is true that if one takes into consideration such factors as heredity, education and social background, the personal responsibility of those in power is much reduced and perhaps even nonexistent. But then if the king is not responsible for his commissions and omissions; if in spite of the oppression, the dispossession, and the massacre of the people carried out in his name, he should have continued to occupy the highest place in the country, why ever then should Bresci have to pay with a life of indescribable suffering, for an act which, however mistaken some may judge it, no one can deny was inspired by altruistic intentions?

But this business of seeking to place the responsibility where it belongs is only of secondary interest to us.

3.   *l'Agitazione*, September 22, 1901

We do not believe in the right to punish; we reject the idea of revenge as a barbarous sentiment. We have no intention of being either executioners or avengers. It seems to us that the role of liberators and peacemakers is more noble and positive. To kings, oppressors and exploiters we would willingly extend our hand, if only they wished to become men among other men, equals among equals.But so long as they insist on profiting from the situation as it exists and to defend it with force, thus causing the martyrdom, the wretchedness and the death through hardships of millions of human beings, we are obliged, we have a duty to oppose force with force ...

We know that these attentats, with the people insufficiently prepared for them, are sterile and often, by provoking reactions which one is unable to control, produce much sorrow, and harm the very cause they were intended to serve.

We know that what is essential and undoubtedly useful is not just to kill a king, the man, but to kill all kings – those of the Courts, of parliaments and of the factories – in the hearts and minds of the people; that is, to uproot faith in the principle of authority to which most people owe allegiance.[4]

I do not need to repeat my disapproval and horror for attentats such as that of the *Diana*, which besides being bad in themselves are also stupid, because they inevitably harm the cause they would wish to serve. And I have never failed to protest strongly, whenever similar acts have taken place and especially when it has turned out that they have been committed by authentic anarchists. I have protested when it would have been better for me to remain silent, because my protest was inspired by superior reasons of principles and tactics, and because I had a duty to do so, since there are people gifted with little personal critical sense, who allow themselves to be guided by what I say. But now it is not a case of judging the fact, and discussing whether it was a good or bad thing to have done, or whether similar actions should or should not have been repeated. Now it is a question of judging men threatened with a punishment a thousand times worse than the death penalty; and so one must examine who these men are, what were their intentions and the circumstances in which they acted.[5]

4. 'Causa ed Effeti', September 22, 1900
5. *Umanità Nova*, December 18, 1921

... I said that those assassins are *also* saints and heroes; and those of my friends who protest against my statement do so in homage to those whom they call the real saints and heroes, who, it would seem, never make mistakes.

I can do no more than confirm what I said. When I think of all that I have learned about Mariani and Aguggini; when I think what good sons and brothers they were, and what affectionate and devoted comrades they were in everyday life, always ready to take risks and to make sacrifices when there was urgent need, I bemoan their fate, I bemoan the destiny that has turned those fine and noble beings into assassins.

I said that one day they will be praised – I did not say that I would praise them; and they will be praised because, as has happened with so many others, the brutal action, the passion that misled them will be forgotten, and only the idea which inspired them and the martyrdom which made them sacrosanct will be remembered.

I don't want to get involved in historical examples; but I could if I wished find in the history of all conspiracies and revolutions, in that of the Italian Risorgimento as well as in our own, a thousand examples of men who have committed actions as bad and as stupid as that of the Diana and yet who are praised by their respective parties, because in fact one forgets the action and remembers the intention, and the individual becomes a symbol and the event is transformed into a legend.

Yes, there are saints and heroes who are assassins; there are assassins who are saints and heroes.

The human mind is really most complicated, and there is a disequilibrium between what one calls heart and what is called brain, between affective qualities and the intellectual faculties, which produces the most unpredictable results and makes possible the most striking contradictions in human behaviour. The war volunteer inebriated by patriotic propaganda, convinced of serving the cause of justice and civilisation, and prepared for the supreme sacrifice, who raged against the 'enemy' – Italian against Austrian, or vice versa – and died in the act of killing, was undoubtedly a hero, but a hero who was unconsciously an assassin.

Torquemada who tortured others as well as himself to serve God and to save souls, was both a saint and an assassin ...

It could easily be argued that the saint and the hero are almost always unbalanced individuals. But then everything would be reduced to a question of words, to a question of definition. What is a saint? What is a hero?

Enough of hair-splitting.

What is important is to avoid confusing the act with the intentions, and in condemning the bad actions not to overlook doing justice to the good intentions. And not only on the grounds of respect for the truth, or human pity, but also for reasons of propaganda, for the practical repercussions that our judgement may have.

There are, and, so long as present conditions and the environment of violence in which we live last, there will always be generous men, who are rebellious and oversensitive, but who lack sufficient powers of reflection and who in certain situations allow themselves to be carried away by passion and strike out blindly. If we do not openly recognise the goodness of their intentions, if we do not distinguish between error and wickedness, we lose any moral influence over them and abandon them to their blind impulses. If instead, we pay homage to their goodness, their courage and sense of sacrifice, we can reach their minds through their hearts, and ensure that those valuable storehouses of energy shall be used in an intelligent and good, as well as useful, way in the interests of the [common] cause.[6]

6. *Umanità Nova*, December 24, 1921

A new title from FREEDOM PRESS

Social *Defence*
Social Change

Brian Martin

FREEDOM PRESS

158pp   ISBN 0 900384 69 7   £4.95